FLAWED BUT FAITHFUL
HOW THE WORST SINNERS MADE HEAVEN'S HALL OF FAME

BY MARK DRISCOLL

Flawed But Faithful: How the Worst Sinners Made Heaven's Hall of Fame
© 2025 by Mark Driscoll

ISBN: 978-1-966223-22-1 (Hard cover), 978-1-966223-23-8 (Paperback), 978-1-966223-24-5 (E-book)

Unless otherwise indicated, scripture quotations are from The Holy Bible, English Standard Version, copyright 2001 by Crossway Bibles, a publishing ministry of Good News Publishers. Used by permission. All rights reserved.

All emphases in Scripture quotations have been added by the author.

No part of this publication may be reproduced, stored in a retrieval system, or transmitted in any form by any means, electronic, mechanical, photocopy, recording, or otherwise, without the prior permission of the publisher, except as provided for by USA copyright law.

CONTENTS

More Resources

About Pastor Mark Driscoll & RealFaith   1

1. Faith, Failure, and our Faithful God (11:1-3)   4
2. Faith for Abel (11:4)   26
3. Faith for Enoch (11:5-6)   36
4. Faith for Noah (11:7)   46
5. Faith for Abraham and Sarah (11:8-16)   54
6. Faith for Isaac (11:17-20)   70
7. Faith for Jacob (11:21)   82
8. Faith for Joseph (11:22)   90
9. Faith for Moses (11:23-29)   102
10. Faith for Joshua (11:30)   118
11. Faith for Rahab (11:31)   132
12. Faith for Barak (11:32)   144
13. Faith for Gideon (11:32)   154
14. Faith for Jephthah (11:32)   164
15. Faith for Samson (11:32)   172
16. Faith for David (11:32)   182
17. Faith for Samuel (11:32)   194
18. Faith for the Prophets (11:32-40)   202

DOWNLOAD THE NEW REALFAITH+ APP TO GET EXCLUSIVE CONTENT FROM PASTOR MARK & GRACE.

WANT TO STUDY THE ENTIRE BOOK OF HEBREWS? GET THE STUDY GUIDE BUNDLE HERE.

ABOUT PASTOR MARK DRISCOLL & REALFAITH

Pastor Mark is a bold, unapologetic Bible teacher with a master's in theology. He is a sought-after preacher and public speaker and has authored over 60 books and study guides, including popular titles like *New Days Old Demons*, *Act Like a Man*, and *King of Kings*.

Pastor Mark and Grace have served in ministry together since 1993 and have raised five kids who love and serve Jesus. Today, Pastor Mark is the Founding and Senior Pastor of Trinity Church in Scottsdale, Arizona, where four generations of his family serve Jesus together. Having become grandparents, they love nothing more than to spend their free time being grandpa and grandma, also known as Bop Bop and Nana.

Pastor Mark and Grace founded RealFaith together with their daughter Ashley in 2016. At RealFaith, it's all about changing lives with practical truth. From best-selling books to viral sermons to in-depth classes and videos, their Bible-based resources help hundreds of millions of people around the globe each year to deepen their faith, love their families, and leave a legacy. If you'd like to learn more, visit **RealFaith.com** or download the new **RealFaith app**. If you have any prayer requests or a testimony regarding how God has used this and other resources to help you learn God's Word, we would love to hear from you at **hello@realfaith.com**.

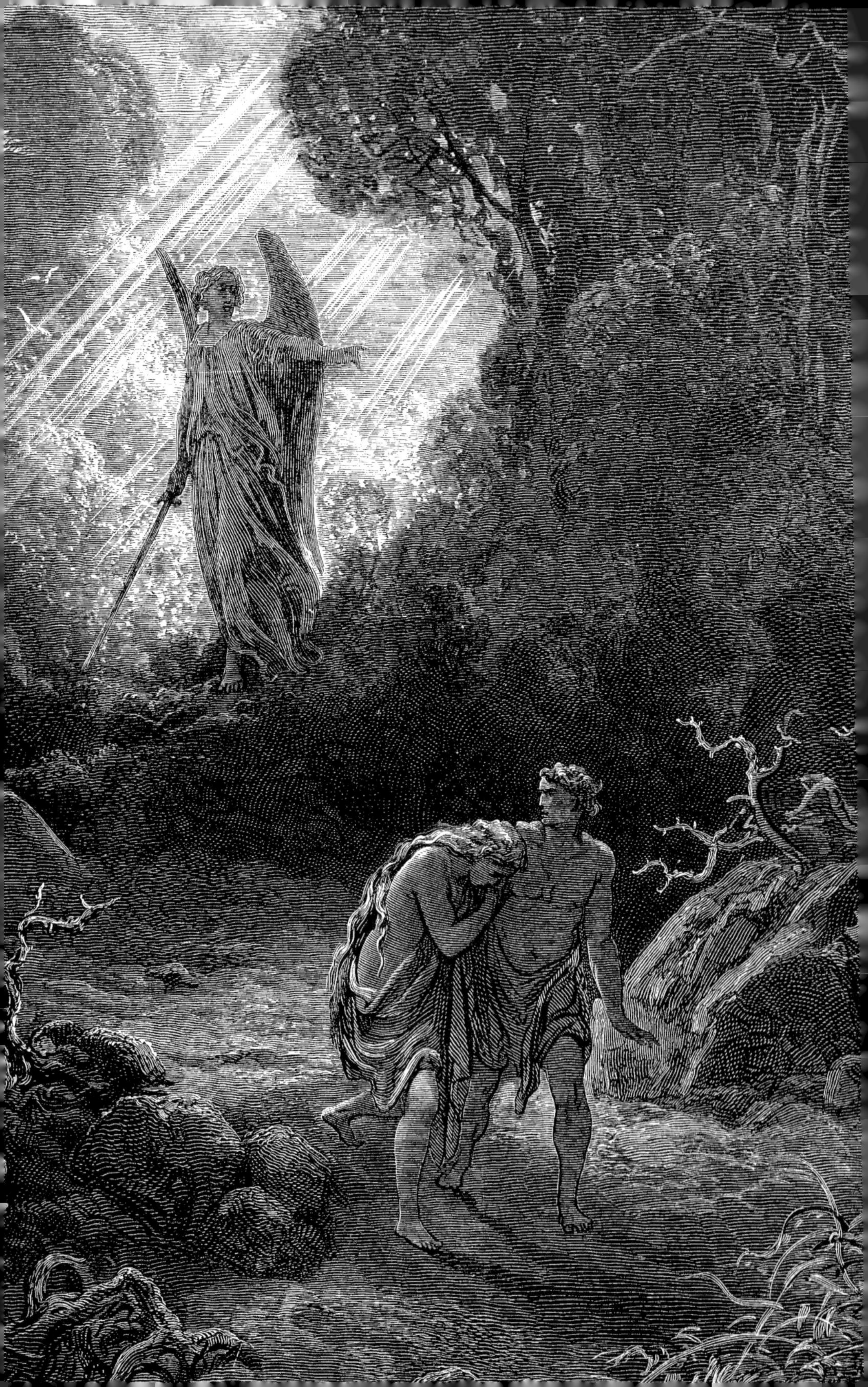

MAN VS GOD

Chapter 1: Faith, Failure, and our Faithful God
Hebrews 11:1-3

Hebrews 11:1-3 – Now faith is the assurance of things hoped for, the conviction of things not seen. For by it the people of old received their commendation. By faith we understand that the universe was created by the word of God, so that what is seen was not made out of things that are visible.

Faith.

This little word has shaped the world. Throughout human history, people in every culture have had some form of faith—a deep commitment to someone or something that is divine and beyond themselves. Various religious and spiritual belief systems are referred to as varying "faiths."

Within faiths, there are heroes of that faith that inspire other followers of that faith by their incredible faith. People with extraordinary faith are celebrated for trusting even when there was no hope and suffering for their faith as martyrs, and their faith stories are retold as heroic and legendary inspiration for others to follow.

What is faith? Who, or what, should be the object of trust we are putting our faith in? How can we increase our faith? Does our faith help determine the outcome of our lives, with more faith moving the needle of positive outcome for our life in our preferred direction? These are the kinds of questions, debates, and discussions that people of varying faiths have had in every generation.

The most significant faith tradition in world history is Christianity. More people are committed to Jesus Christ as the object of their faith than anyone or anything in the history of the world. Today, a few billion people on the earth claim the Christian faith, and the Church of Jesus Christ is the biggest movement of any sort or kind in world history—spanning more nations, races, cultures, languages, and generations than any government, religion, or philosophy.

The great Bible preacher Charles Spurgeon said,

Without faith we are without God, for God is only apprehended by faith. Without faith we are without hope, for a true hope can only spring out of a true faith. Without faith we are without Christ and, consequently, without a Savior. It would be infinitely better to be without eyes, without hearing, without wealth, without bread, without garments, without a home rather than to be without the faith that brings everything the soul requires. Without faith we are spiritually naked, poor, miserable, lost, condemned—and without a hope of escape.[1]

<u>Faith</u>

According to the Christian Scriptures,

> In the OT [Old Testament] and NT [New Testament], "faith" carries several meanings. It may mean simple trust in God or in the Word of God, and at other times faith almost becomes equivalent to active obedience. It may also find expression in the affirmation of a creedal statement. Thus, it also comes to mean the entire body of received Christian teaching or truth—"the truth."[2]

Hebrews 11 is widely considered the greatest chapter in the Bible about faith. While we do not know who wrote Hebrews, when it was written, or which church originally received it to be read aloud in their assembly, we do know that Hebrews 11 reads unlike any other chapter in the entire book. A Bible handbook says, "This chapter is the best-known part of Hebrews and generally the easiest to understand. It is also to some extent different from anything else in the letter.[3]

Throughout the history of the Christian Church, Hebrews 11 has also been esteemed as one of the richest and most beloved chapters in all of Scripture. The following are some of the most moving and compelling comments on Hebrews 11 from scholars:

- "...famous and moving..., eloquent and majestic."[4&5]

- "Hebrews 11 has become one of the best-known chapters in Scripture. The heroes and heroines of faith portrayed here make a stirring impact on readers in all generations."[6]
- "Hebrews has now reached a plateau from which there is an excellent view of those who have gone on before. Looking at them, the readers can discover for themselves what is up ahead."[7]
- "This is one of the grand chapters of the Bible, a gallery of notable portraits of ancient great believers, each drawn with a master hand."[8]
- "This chapter calls the roll of the Old Testament heroes of the faith."[9]
- "Hebrews 11, often referred to as the great 'Hall of Faith,' has become through the centuries one of the church's most-loved portions of Scripture. Poetic in its cadence, panoramic in its historical sweep, and imminently relevant in its challenge, this chapter calls the believer to faithful endurance by use of voluminous testimony from the lives of ancient saints."[10]
- "Hebrews 11 tells us what it means to have faith and obtain life."[11]
- "In chapter 11 we have one of the deservedly famous set pieces of New Testament rhetoric: the roll call of the heroes of faith."[12]

The introduction to Hebrews 11 is found just a few verses prior in 10:22-23: "…let us draw near with a true heart in full assurance of faith…Let us hold fast the confession of our hope without wavering, for he who promised is faithful." Faith is worthless unless the object of faith is faithful. For example, someone on a sinking ship at sea may have one final choice between grabbing onto an anchor instead of a life preserver, with full faith in its' power to save, but they will die because the object of their faith cannot save. Similarly, faith in a false god, demonic spirituality, or atheistic aspiration of nothing beyond the material world all require faith—but that faith is in vain. Only the God of the Bible is a faithful object to place our faith in. Hebrews 10:38-39 then says, "'...my righteous one shall live by faith, and if he shrinks back, my soul has no pleasure in him.' But we are not of those who shrink back and are destroyed, but of those who have faith and preserve their souls." This section quotes Habakkuk 2:4 from the Old Testament, which Paul also quotes in Romans 1:17 and Galatians 3:11 as key to his argument for "justification by faith," which is the heart of the Protestant Reformation's rediscovery of the gospel of grace.

The book of Habakkuk is a series of conversations between the frustrated prophet and God. Much like today, Habakkuk was living at a time of corrupt government, economic anxiety, plagues, racial division, conflict in the streets, and lethargic believers. Habakkuk asks this question: How long? How long was God going to allow chaos and destruction? Then the Lord answers him in Habakkuk 2:4: "...the righteous shall live by faith." They don't live by sight. The righteous know there's a God over all these circumstances. Habakkuk can't see the future himself, but he trusts the God of the future. That's faith.

The theme of Hebrews 11 is "faith," appearing 24 times in 40 verses. The chapter opens with the line, "Now faith is the assurance of things hoped for, the conviction of things not seen." Here, faith is both defined and described according to the Scriptures. A Bible resource says,

> Let us look carefully at the definition. It consists of two parts...First...faith [is] "the substance of things hoped for." Now "things hoped for" are things which have no present subsistence; so far as our enjoyment or possession of them is concerned, they must be future. But "faith,"..."is the substance of things hoped for." It is that which gives a present being to these things. It takes them out of the shadowy region of probability, and brings them into that of actual reality. Faith is, moreover, the "evidence of things not seen." By "things not seen" we understand such as are not to be ascertained to us by our senses, or even by our reason—not seen either by the eye of the body or by the far more powerful eye of the mind. These are

the truths and facts revealed to us by the Word of God, and of which, independently on that Word, we must have remained wholly ignorant. Its province is with invisible things, and of these it is "the evidence"—the demonstration, or conviction...[13]

Faith: An Internal Conviction and External Action

When our five kids were little, we repeated the same scene at some point in each of their lives. I would be in a pool, standing up in water to my chest, and they would be standing on the edge, wanting to jump in but scared. I would look them in the eye, smile, and lovingly ask them, "Do you trust your dad?" They would reply "Yes," with varying degrees of confidence. I would then say, "If you trust your dad, jump in the pool and I will catch you."

This is the kind of faith that Christian philosopher Søren Kierkegaard (1813–55) said was necessary for believers. He referred to a "leap of faith" to prove "that genuine faith involves not intellectual certainty but risk or a leap of faith by which one commits one's whole being without certainties."[14]

Sometimes, faith means sitting still, waiting for God to show up, and saying and doing nothing. Other times, faith means getting up, activating, and putting your faith into action.

For purposes of our study of Hebrews 11, biblical faith is this: *Faith is a Holy Spirit-empowered internal devotion to God (faith) that produces an external devotion to God (obedient works or fruit)*. Internal devotion to God is what God sees. God alone knows who has saving faith.

When our faith is revealed in external actions, we are serving as a witness to others, and our obedience is part of our testimony. This is the backdrop of those people mentioned in Hebrews 11. For example, Noah's internal faith produced an external action when he built the Ark. Abraham and Sarah's internal faith produced an external action when they left their families and homeland to follow a God they barely knew to a place He had not yet revealed. Abraham's family's internal faith produced an external action when they moved from their home to Egypt in the days of Joseph in fulfillment of a previous prophecy given over their family. Moses' internal faith produced external action when he repeatedly told King Pharaoh that plagues were coming from God in divine judgment and led a nation of slaves into freedom through the Red Sea, which was miraculously parted as they walked into the waters by faith. Joshua's internal faith produced external action when he led a generation of God's people into the Promised Land through a river at flood stage that needed to part; otherwise they would drown. Rahab's internal faith produced external action when she risked her life to spare God's people. The internal faith of the Judges—Gideon, Barak, Samson, and Jephthah—produced external action as they each led much smaller and weaker armies to massive defeats of the enemies of God. The internal faith of David produced external action when he took down the giant Goliath as a shepherd boy with a slingshot. Samuel and the prophets' faith internally produced a fearless resolve externally to speak the Word of God against sinful authorities that included kings and kingdoms, knowing their preaching was a declaration of war.

Too often, Christians will use faith to excuse laziness, inactivity, and cowardice. Real faith requires risk and action and comes with a heavy dose of anxiety much of the time. Faith is not safe, and it is sometimes a leap of obedience to the Word of God. Faith does not merely sit on the couch trusting God to provide. As Hebrews 11 reveals, oftentimes, real faith gets up off the couch to build an ark, move to another nation, lead a people into the destiny God has for them, have a head-on collision with evil, or fight for the truth of God no matter what the cost. Faith is not just what you believe; faith is also how you behave. Faith is not just what you feel; faith is also what you do. Faith does not just live in your heart; faith also takes over your life. A Bible handbook provides the following helpful summary of how those people in Hebrews 11 had their internal faith revealed in their external action:

- Abel's faith: he offered the first sacrifice for sin made by faith and not works (Hebrews 11:4; Genesis 4:1–15).

- Enoch's faith: he walked with God, pleased Him, and was taken away by Him (Hebrews 11:5–6; Genesis 5:22, 24).
- Noah's faith: he kept on building the Ark when nobody thought there would be any use for it (Hebrews 11:7; Genesis 6:14–22).
- Abraham's faith: he set out to find the city of God without knowing where it was; he was willing to offer his son as a sacrifice, in confidence that God would bring him back to life (Hebrews 11:8–12, 17–19; Genesis 12:1–7; Gen. 22).
- Sarah's faith: she came to believe what she at first had laughed at as impossible (Hebrews 11:11–12; Genesis 17:19; 18:11–14).
- Isaac's faith: he foretold the future by faith (Hebrews 11:20; Genesis 27:27–29).
- Jacob's faith: he believed that God would fulfill His promises (Hebrews 11:21; Genesis 49).
- Joseph's faith: he believed that his bones would rest in Canaan (Hebrews 11:22; Genesis 50:25).
- Moses' faith: he chose to suffer with Israel and turned his back on Egypt; he kept the Passover; he crossed the Red Sea; he saw Him who is invisible (Hebrews 11:23–29; Exodus 2:2–11; 12:21, 50; 14:22–29).
- Joshua's faith: it made the walls of Jericho fall (Hebrews 11:30; Joshua 6:20).
- Rahab's faith: she cast her lot with Israel (Hebrews 11:31; Joshua 2:9; 6:23).
- Gideon's faith: he became mighty in war (Hebrews 11:32; Judges 7:21).
- Barak's faith: he subdued kingdoms (Hebrews 11:32; Judges 4).
- Samson's faith: his weakness was turned into strength (Hebrews 11:32, 34; Judges 16:28).
- Jephthah's faith: he defeated armies (Hebrews 11:32, 34; Judges 11).
- David's faith: he obtained promises (Hebrews 11:32–33; 2 Samuel 7:11–13).
- Daniel's faith: he stopped the mouths of lions (Hebrews

11:32–33; Daniel 6:22).
- Jeremiah's faith: he was tortured for his faith (Hebrews 11:32, 35; Jeremiah 20:2).
- Elijah's faith: he raised the dead (Hebrews 11:32, 35; 1 Kings 17:17–24).
- Elisha's faith: he raised the dead (Hebrews 11:32, 35; 2 Kings 4:8–37).
- Zechariah's faith: he was stoned for his faith (Hebrews 11:32, 37; 2 Chronicles 24:20–21).
- Isaiah's faith: he was sawed in two for his faith, according to tradition (Hebrews 11:32, 37).[15]

Faith in Hebrews 11

In Hebrews 11, we find a list of well-known Old Testament characters, with their lives being presented as an example of faith in God. When taught, the chapter often presents these people much like superheroes—men and women who overcame insurmountable odds with their fortitude welded into place by their unwavering trust in God to do the impossible, which He does! The chapter is often referred to as the "Hall of Faith," or "Hall of Fame," or, as one Bible commentary says, "Learning Faith from the Champions!"

In this study of Hebrews 11, we will take a different approach. I spent most of a year preaching through Hebrews and saved chapter 11 for last. There is a tendency in everything from religion to politics to present the best days of the lives of our heroes and ignore their worst days. Conversely, the enemies of our heroes do the exact opposite—highlighting their worst days as a leader and neglecting their best days. Something in us wants to idolize our heroes and demonize others. I was raised Catholic, and in that faith tradition, the saints loom large. Those with extraordinary faith are venerated by the Church and extolled as heroes. With less formality, we Protestants do the same when we fail to mention that our Reformation heroes like John Calvin had a man killed over a theological disagreement and Martin Luther said some very antisemitic things against the Jews that Adolf Hitler later weaponized for the Holocaust. The same is true of our political leaders, as we overlook a mountain of flaws to support a candidate for office while celebrating any good they have done or might do.

To be fair, the people mentioned in Hebrews 11 saw God show up in supernatural and history-altering ways. These men and women trusted God for the impossible, and we need to learn from their faith. However, those listed in Hebrews 11 also are very human, with some very real faults, flaws, and failures.

<u>Failure</u>

What I have always taught our kids, now our grandkids, and people in our church is that we need to be honest. Christianity is not a public relations firm committed to personal brand creation and reputation management. Christianity is an ongoing radical commitment of sinners to be honestly repentant about their sins and need for God to save them not just from Satan, sin, death, and Hell—but also themselves.

As we study Hebrews 11, we will examine both the faith of those mentioned and also their faithlessness. These people showed extraordinary faith on their best days but also ordinary faithlessness on their worst days. The people God uses over and over in the Bible are, at times, very flawed, failing people. While their faith is not perfect, their God, who is the object of it, is perfect. Therefore, the hero of the Bible, and everyone in it, along with all of us who have been saved by believing in its' gospel message about Jesus Christ, is our faithful God. As 2 Timothy 2:13 says, "…if we are faithless, he remains faithful…" It's not faith that delivers but God who delivers. This explains why Noah is honored, even though he got drunk and passed out naked in his tent like a hillbilly on vacation in the woods. Abraham is honored, despite giving away the promised wife twice and the Promised Land once. Sarah is honored, despite encouraging Abraham to practice polygamy and impregnate a servant girl, which has led to an ongoing bloody family feud between Jews and Arab Muslims, who are both convinced their family line are the heirs of the promises of the Abrahamic

Covenant. Abraham's family is honored, even though Isaac gave away his wife and played favorites with his sons just like his father and even though Jacob is a momma's boy who tricks his brother Esau out of the family birthright, flees as a coward, and gets abused by his father-in-law for over a decade, ultimately marrying sisters and working basically as a slave until he gets a backbone and stands up for himself and his family. Moses murdered a man, was not, at first, a willing servant of God, and got so angry he broke the first copy of the 10 Commandments God carved in stone for him; ultimately, he was not allowed to enter the Promised Land after 40 years of wilderness wandering because of his sin. Joshua erred on a few occasions, making major decisions for the nation without consulting God, which caused him to overlook sin among the men, leading to a brutal military defeat. Rahab was both a prostitute and a liar. Gideon fathered many sons with a parade of women who were nearly all murdered by a jealous brother; Barak was a weak and timid man, which forced Deborah to step up as the senior national leader; Samson was known for drinking, gambling, and sleeping with prostitutes; and Jephthah made a rash vow to God, which ended up in him murdering his own daughter. David committed adultery and murdered the woman's husband, Samuel sinned when he left his godless "worthless" sons in ministry leadership, and the rest of the Old Testament prophets' sins include, at times, being cowards and siding with God's enemies.

When we fail to act in faith, what the Bible also calls faithlessness, we become unfaithful to God through sin, causing failure. Even the most devout people in the Bible and human history have experienced these doubt-filled days. On those days, God is still faithful. Even when someone is unfaithful to God, He remains faithful: "Does their faithlessness nullify the faithfulness of God? By no means!"[a]

In our study of those saints of God mentioned in Hebrews 11, we will examine three things: 1) the faith of God's people 2) the failures of God's people 3) God's faithfulness. The goal is not to idolize or demonize God's servants but rather to be as

[a] Romans 3:3-4

honest as the Bible is so that we see God doing extraordinary things through ordinary people like us, giving us hope and faith that He can use us for His purposes, despite our imperfections. The good news of Hebrews 11 is that God does perfect work through imperfect people.

Our Faithful God

In the opening line of the Bible, we read, "In the beginning, God…" God is the author, center, and hero of the Bible. The Bible is for you, but it is not primarily about you. The first and most important thing for you to learn is who God is. Until you know who God is, you cannot understand who you are, where you come from, why you exist, what the purpose of your life is, or where you are going when you die.

You were made by God to be in relationship with God, living to glorify God, and will die and stand before God. Today, your faith must be in the One True God, or it is in vain.

Hebrews 11 (v.3) begins by echoing Genesis 1:1, "By faith we understand that the universe was created by the word of God, so that what is seen was not made out of things that are visible."

What the author of Hebrews is saying is simple but profound: everything begins with faith. He begins by using creation as a case study in faith—none of us were there as an eyewitness, so we cannot claim to know exactly how the world came into being. Furthermore, the scientific method of testing and retesting a hypothesis in a controlled environment is impossible with creation, as well as other miracles, for the very reason that they are one-time events that are non-repeatable. The point is simply this—there are numerous things that we can only understand by faith, and many of them are the most important matters of life, such as where we and the world came from, who God is, and what happens after we die. For example, the person who says that the material world brought order out of chaos by random chance assumes something they also cannot prove. The atheist who denies there is a God or that, as Creator, He designed the world in which we live, has faith that their mind functions properly—something they cannot prove without using their mind. Faith is presupposing something is true and trusting it, even though you cannot prove it. Psalm 14:11 says of the atheist's presupposition, "The fool says in his heart, 'There is no God.'" A presupposition is "an idea that is assumed or taken for granted, rather than proven.[16]

In philosophy, there is an entire approach to understanding and defending the Christian faith called *presuppositionalism*, which is

> [a] term describing a particular approach to philosophy and theology, it argues that all systems of knowledge are founded on unprovable assumptions about God, human nature and reality. Theoretical thought must, therefore, begin with a conscious appraisal of these assumptions. In this view, claims of objectivity as found in empiricism, rationalism or scientism are little more than pretensions resting on unexamined assumptions.[17]

Every belief system has, as its foundation, a faith assumption, or a presupposition. For example, in 1962, historian and philosopher of science Thomas Kuhn, who originally studied as a physicist at Harvard, laid out a radically new conception of scientific discovery in his landmark book, *The Structure of Scientific Revolutions*. He showed that scientific progress is not linear through research and data; instead, the world of science is completely overturned when a new presupposition, or faith assumption, is laid in place of one previously held so that there is a new "paradigm," or worldview, through which to interpret all data and experience.

For example, the atheist presupposes there is no God and constructs an entire worldview upon that unprovable faith assumption. A worldview is literally a lens through which a person views all of life and interprets all data. This reasoning explains why the atheist does not believe in God, angels, demons, or the human soul—because they presuppose that there is only a physical world and nothing spiritual beyond the material. Furthermore, they presuppose, by faith, that their mind functions in accordance with reality, something they cannot prove but also have to trust.

However, the Christian begins by presupposing there is a God, and our highest priority should be knowing, trusting, loving, and obeying Him. The atheist cannot prove their faith presupposition that there is no God. However, the Christian who believes in Jesus Christ is trusting in the only founder of any major world religion who claimed to be God and said they would rise from death to prove it. Our faith presupposes that Jesus Christ is God.

Hebrews 11:1-3 says of the Christian,

> Now faith is the assurance of things hoped for, the conviction of things not seen. For by it the people of old received their commendation. By faith we understand that the universe was created by the word of God, so that what is seen was not made out of things that are visible.

Hebrews 11:6 says, "…without faith it is impossible to please him, for whoever would draw near to God must believe that he exists and that he rewards those who seek him."

In the opening lines of Hebrews 11, which serve as the foundation and definition of faith, there are five things we learn about creation:

One, faith "is the assurance of things hoped for." Faith is about the future, whereas sight is about the present or past. When we look into the future, our options are fear or faith. If we choose fear when looking into the future, it causes anxiety in the present as we anticipate that the days ahead are dark or even dangerous. Conversely, if we look into the future with faith instead of fear, we do not merely look at the people and obstacles against us but also the God who is the Creator of all. Our God is bigger than anyone or anything that looms large in our future, and faith allows us to trust He will be good for His promises to bless us as He did the list of those He protected and provided for in Hebrews 11.

Two, faith is "the conviction of things not seen." The word "conviction" is also sometimes translated as the English word "evidence," bringing to mind courtroom imagery with a legal tone. It refers to that which provides proof through testing or demonstration. In this sense, faith is not irrational belief but the perceptive grasp of that which cannot be seen. One Bible scholar says, "Faith is looking at God and trusting him for everything, when all we have is his word."[18]

Sight is how we see the seen realm of the physical world in which we live, and faith is how we see the unseen realm of the spiritual world in which we also live. A Bible commentator says,

> Eyesight produces a conviction about objects in the physical world. Faith produces the same convictions for the invisible order. Faith shows itself by producing assurance that what we hope for will happen. Faith also provides an insight into realities which otherwise remain unseen. A person with faith lets these unseen realities from God provide a living, effective power for daily life.[19]

Three, faith is how "people of old received their commendation." This principle establishes the theme for the remainder of Hebrews 11, which serves as a commendation and commentary on how God's people in the Old Testament lived by faith in their faithful God. From generation to generation, the one thing that God rewards is faith in Him. This is the point and purpose for Hebrews 11—not merely to admire the faith of Old Testament saints but to also emulate it and be rewarded as they were. The Church Father Augustine [354-430 AD] said,

> The reason faith is greatly rewarded is that it does not see and yet believes. I mean, if it could see, what reward would there be?...But faith does not falter, because it is supported by hope. Take away hope, and faith falters. How, after all, when you are walking somewhere, will you even move your feet, if you have no hope of ever getting there? If, though, from each of them, that is from faith and hope, you withdraw love, what is the point of believing; what is the point of hoping, if you do not love? Indeed, you cannot

even hope for anything you do not love. Love, you see, kindles hope; hope shines through love.[20]

Four, faith is how "we understand that the universe was created by the word of God..." The author of Hebrews establishes the Scriptures as the very words of God—perfect and in the highest authority, as God cannot lie. Earlier in the book, Hebrews 4:12–13 said,

> For the word of God is living and active, sharper than any two-edged sword, piercing to the division of soul and of spirit, of joints and of marrow, and discerning the thoughts and intentions of the heart. And no creature is hidden from his sight, but all are naked and exposed to the eyes of him to whom we must give account.

The Word of God is central throughout Hebrews as "he upholds the universe by the word of his power."[a] God's Word is to be trusted and obeyed: "Today, if you hear his voice, do not harden your hearts."[b] Hearing and heeding the Word of God is how we mature in faith, "for everyone who lives on milk is unskilled in the word of righteousness, since he is a child."[c] To become a believer with faith in Christ includes having "tasted the goodness of the word of God and the powers of the age to come..."[d] The entire point of the Bible is faith in Jesus Christ, who "speaks a better word..."[e] Christian leaders in the church are known as "those who spoke to you the word of God."[f] Lastly, the only way to have faith, sustain faith, and grow in faith is to "bear with [the] word of exhortation..."[g]

Five, faith is how we learn and mature because "what is seen was not made out of things that are visible." The opening line of Scripture clearly reveals that creation comes from God.[h] Genesis 1-2 further reveals God as a prophet who both made creation and prepared it for us solely by the power of His word. This is indicated by the repeated phrases "And God said" and "Let there be" or "Let the..."[i] When God spoke,

---

[a] Hebrews 1:3 [b] Hebrews 4:7 [c] Hebrews 5:13 [d] Hebrews 6:5 [e] Hebrews 12:24 [f] Hebrews 13:7 [g] Hebrews 13:22 [h] Genesis 1:1 [i] Genesis 1:3, 6, 9, 11, 14, 20, 24, 26

creation obeyed His command, as is repeatedly demonstrated by the phrase, "And it was so." After each act of creating, God pronounced the perfectly sinless nature of His creation with the phrase "And God saw that it was good."

The Bible teaches that God made creation *ex nihilo* (Latin for "out of nothing"). Hebrews 11:3 says, "By faith we understand that the universe was created by the word of God, so that what is seen was not made out of things that are visible." This doctrine is important because it negates the possibility of naturalistic evolution and an eternal universe. While God did not make creation from any preexisting matter or the proverbial hunk of mud, creation did come into existence and was prepared for human inhabitation by the powerful word of God.

Therefore, original creation came not from preexisting matter but rather out of nothing, by God's word. We are to trust God by faith, and faith trusts the Word of God.

God did not create from nothing on each of the six days of creation. Still, God did speak as both a prophet and poet on each day. Furthermore, there is a set pattern to God's words in Genesis 1 as the foundation of our faith:

1. Announcement: "And God said."
2. Commandment: "Let there be."
3. Separation: God separated the day and night, water and land, animals, and plants.
4. Report: "And it was so."
5. Evaluation: "And God saw that it was good."

In this pattern we see that God's word is living, active, and powerful and that it accomplishes what He decrees. Isaiah 55:11 says, "[S]o shall my word be that goes out from my mouth; it shall not return to me empty, but it shall accomplish that which I purpose, and shall succeed in the thing for which I sent it." The rest of Scripture confirms that creation was prepared for us by God's powerful word.[a]

Genesis 1 portrays God's word as the most powerful force

---

[a] Psalm 33:6, 9; 148:5; 2 Pet. 3:7

in all of creation. God's word brings order, makes things good, creates an environment in which life can exist, separates things, comes with unparalleled authority, and accomplishes exactly what God intends. Therefore, we are not to dismiss, disdain, or distort God's word, as it is the source of understanding.

<u>Pushing Through the Pain</u>

New levels of pain require new levels of faith. As new trials, temptations, and troubles come, facing them requires new, fresh, and deeper faith in the Word of God and His character. This is true in your life and is the backdrop for the entire book of Hebrews.

Just prior to the exhortation for fresh faith in Hebrews 11, Hebrews 10:32–36 talks about the struggling and suffering they were experiencing:

> But recall the former days when, after you were enlightened, you endured a hard struggle with sufferings, sometimes being publicly exposed to reproach and affliction, and sometimes being partners with those so treated. For you had compassion on those in prison, and you joyfully accepted the plundering of your property, since you knew that you yourselves had a better possession and an abiding one. Therefore do not throw away your confidence, which has a great reward. For you have need of endurance, so that when you have done the will of God you may receive what is promised.

There will be times that you will need to pay a high price to remain in right relationship with Jesus Christ; in those times, you need to remind yourself of the highest price He paid to be in relationship with you. Over and over, Hebrews reminds us of Jesus shedding His own blood and sacrificing Himself in your place for your sins.

There is a category of people called apostates, which are people who appear to be with and for Christ but then turn and become indifferent to or even anti-Christ. Jesus' disciple

Judas Iscariot serves as a sober warning about apostasy. When the pressure of life squeezes us like a vice, the options are apostasy or deeper faith that enables us to endure more pain and remain steadfast to our Lord no matter what the cost. These new seasons of bewilderment, exhaustion, confusion, loss, or injustice are the reason for the five warning passages throughout Hebrews. Hebrews is filled with warnings against apostasy, exhorting believers to not give up or give in on the hardest days but rather to make a steadfast and resolute commitment to growing in faith:

- Warning 1: Do not abandon God's Word[a]
- Warning 2: Do not become hard-hearted and start ignoring God[b]
- Warning 3: Do not settle for being spiritually immature and stop growing[c]
- Warning 4: Do not become disloyal and turn your back on Jesus Christ[d]
- Warning 5: Do not reject God's Word and His authority over your life[e]

In some ways, faith is like a muscle. Athletic trainers say that the key to strengthening a muscle is resistance training. The more you push back against weight and pressure, the stronger you become. At first, this seems painful and not worthwhile. However, if you push through the pain, you become stronger, healthier, more resilient, and better prepared to overcome whoever or whatever comes against you in the future. This is precisely what Hebrews 12:11 means as a follow-up to this great chapter on faith, saying, "For the moment all discipline seems painful rather than pleasant, but later it yields the peaceful fruit of righteousness to those who have been trained by it."

This is the goal of learning from the example of those listed in Hebrews 11 who endured in faith. We will begin our study of that chapter and the lives of these people next with the hope of

[a] Hebrews 2:1-4 [b] Hebrews 3:7-4:13 [c] Hebrews 5:11-6:12 [d] Hebrews 10:19-39
[e] Hebrews 12:14-29

exercising faith so that we grow stronger in trusting the Lord.

Dig Deeper.
1. Read Habakkuk 2:4, which is a mega-verse in the Bible about faith.
2. Read the verses and surrounding context where the New Testament quotes Habakkuk 2:4: Romans 1:17; Galatians 3:11; Hebrews 10:38-39.
3. Carefully read all of Hebrews 11 to prepare to learn it in greater depth as we study it.

Walk it out. Talk it out.
1. Take a few minutes and have everyone in the group share a brief summary of their faith journey.
2. What "leap of faith" or action that involved risk has God called you to at some point in your life, including this present season?
3. What are you most hoping to learn as you study Hebrews 11?
4. How can group members be praying for each other this week?

HEBREWS 11

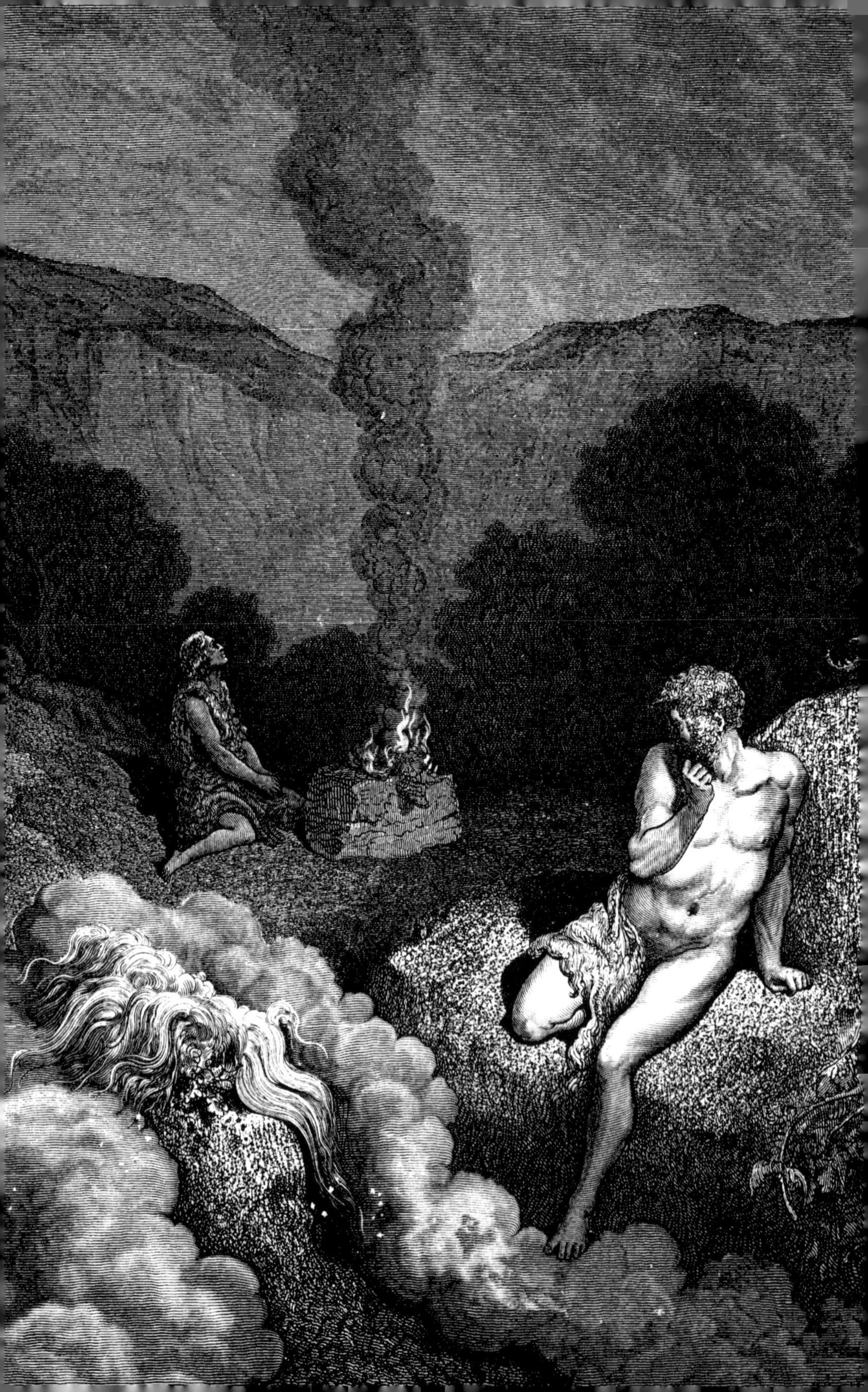

ABEL

Chapter 2: Faith for Abel
Hebrews 11:4

Hebrews 11:4 – By faith Abel offered to God a more acceptable sacrifice than Cain, through which he was commended as righteous, God commending him by accepting his gifts. And through his faith, though he died, he still speaks.

When non-Christians share their life story, it is a biography. When Christians share their life story, it is supposed to be a testimony. The difference between a biography and a testimony is who the hero of the story is. In a biography, there is a tendency to downplay or even dismiss the faults, flaws, and failures of a person honored as a hero. In a testimony, the goal is to be honest about the best and worst days, deeds, and decisions of a person so that God is glorified for His faithfulness to and through them.

Hebrews 11 is a series of testimonies. Each story about the life of one of God's servants is intended to serve as an example and motivation for us and increase our faith to trust God no matter what. The testimonies in Hebrews 11 begin in the first book of the Bible—Genesis.

The word "Genesis" literally means "beginning." The first book of the Bible is literally the genesis, or beginning, of God's revelation to us about who He is and who we are, as well as the beginning of faith. In the first two chapters of Genesis, God makes everyone and everything. In Genesis 3, our first parents sinned against God, siding with Satan in the war against God, and the promise is given that Jesus is coming to defeat sin and deliver sinners. In Genesis 4, we then read about the beginning of faith, starting with the first siblings, Cain and Abel. Adam and Eve had no sin nature when God created them, but as soon as they sinned, the nature was passed on from generation to generation. Romans 5:12-21 explains how Adam's sin nature was passed on to everyone born since. None of us is born naturally good or morally neutral. This is why we need to be born again. As the children of Adam and Eve, the first people born in human history, Cain and Abel were born with a sin nature. Sin is not only something that we do but also someone that we are.

Abel's Faith

Genesis 4 is the beginning of church, where two people come into God's presence and worship Him with the things in their hands. This is a sacrifice, also called an offering. Without the written Scriptures, the law is written on the hearts of Cain and Abel, and they know two things: they need to be in God's presence, and they need to come with an offering or a sacrifice. No one in the Bible comes to worship empty-handed; worship always includes an offering to the Lord.

When we come to worship God, we need to examine two things. First, we need to search what is in our hands. On this point, Cain does better than most Christians—he, at least, brings an offering to the Lord. Many Christians come to worship every week empty-handed, not giving generously to the Lord, so they are worse than Cain on this point. Secondly, we need to search what is in our hearts. Are we coming to listen to the sermon or critique the preacher, singing songs from the heart or just going through the motions, living in forgiveness and grace with those around us or harboring bitterness and unholy anger?

Both Cain and Abel each bring an offering from their vocation. The difference is that one will be accepted, and one will be rejected. Why? The difference was not what they had in their hands but rather what they had in their hearts. An academic Bible resource says of the original Greek word translated into English as "sacrifice here…emphasizes not merely the object given, but the worshipful intent behind it. Faith is not measured by ritual, but by heart-aligned obedience."[21]

Reporting the beginning of ungodly anger, "…Cain was very angry, and his face fell. The Lord said to Cain, 'Why are you angry? And why has your face fallen? If you do well, will you not be accepted? And if you do not do well, sin is crouching at the door. Its desire is contrary to you, but you must rule over it.'"[a]

The Bible says, "...man looks on the outward appearance, but the LORD looks on the heart."[b] Two people can come to church—one filled with greed, pride, and jealousy and the other filled with love for God—and you can't tell the difference just by looking at them. But God can, because He sees the heart. Worship is not just what we do on the outside, but it's also who we are on the inside.

When it came to their hearts, there was a big difference between Cain and Abel. Hebrews 11:4 says, "By faith Abel offered to God a more acceptable sacrifice than Cain, through which he was commended as righteous, God commending him by accepting his gifts. And through his faith, though he died, he still speaks."

One pastor has a great analogy: "Before the Bible is binoculars for them, it must be a mirror for us." We often read the Bible and say, "What was wrong with Cain?" But we need to ask, "What is wrong with me?" Have you ever come to church with a hard heart? We all have. Ultimately, you and I need to search our own hearts and allow God to do the same: "Search me, O God, and know my heart! Try me and know my thoughts! And see if there be any grievous way in me, and lead me in the way everlasting!"[c]

Cain's Failure

Cain murders Abel, the Bible's first martyr, in the Bible's first death. God then asks Cain, "Where is Abel your brother?" Cain responds, "...am I my brother's keeper?"[d] In other words, "Am I his babysitter? Am I his designated driver? It's not my job." Of course, the Lord knows what Cain did, and He pronounces Cain's punishment.

1 John 3:12-13 compares and contrasts these brothers, saying, "We should not be like Cain, who was of the evil one and murdered his brother. And why did he murder him? Because his own deeds were evil and his brother's righteous. Do

[a] Genesis 4:5-7 [b] 1 Samuel 16:7 [c] Psalm 139:23-24 [d] Genesis 4:9

not be surprised, brothers, that the world hates you." The same Satan that came for Adam and Eve came for Cain. What was going on behind the scenes was demonic and spiritual warfare.

Why did Cain murder Abel? "Because his own deeds were evil and his brother's righteous." If you worship the Lord, don't be surprised if, when you are acting like Abel, the world acts like Cain toward you. Have you ever had family members disown or reject you because you love and serve Jesus? Have friends mocked or maligned you? Sometimes when we get in trouble, it's not for doing the wrong thing but rather for doing the right thing. If we are going to live for God, we can expect the world to be against us. Jesus calls him "righteous Abel," and says his own blood was shed for this reason.[a]

Speaking of people who are like Cain, Jude 1:10–11 says, "[T]hese people blaspheme all that they do not understand, and they are destroyed by all that they, like unreasoning animals, understand instinctively. Woe to them! For they walked in the way of Cain…" Cain has spiritual descendants who follow in his pathway and plan. They cause problems, pains, and perils, but God's people should follow in the footsteps of Abel. We need to worship and serve the Lord wholeheartedly, dealing with what is *in* us, regardless of what is happening *around* us.

Did Abel do something to deserve being murdered? No, he was focused on his relationship with God while Cain was focused on Abel and jealousy towards him for having a "better" heart. The problem wasn't that Abel's sacrifice was outwardly better but rather that his heart was purer.

When someone is very unhealthy and broken, they are often repulsed by health. As Cain comes into God's presence, Abel's presence triggers him. Cain is angry. He's upset, emotional, and doesn't feel comfortable here. He's the problem, but he's religious, so he does what religious people do—he fakes it. Still, there is great sickness in his soul. He hides and pretends until the Lord rebukes him.

Two people can come into the presence of God and have very different reactions and responses. Unhealthy people feel

---

[a] Matthew 23:35

uncomfortable around healthy people. Being around people who are sincerely in love with the Lord can be a very uncomfortable place for those who are religious and faking their relationship with the Lord.

Cain didn't just get angry and slaughter his brother; he took him out into a field, away from God's presence, and killed him there. Evil people will do things when no one is looking that they would never do when someone is looking. Cain is doing the same things that his parents did—trying to hide his sin from the Lord God, who sees and knows all. You can't hide anything from an all-knowing Lord.

God pursues Cain after he kills Abel. Cain isn't looking for God, but God is looking for him. God owes Cain nothing, but in an act of grace, He calls out to him.

The point is this: God has been pursuing you. You are not just a victim of the sin of others. You, too, are a sinner, and you have hidden from the Lord. Genesis is telling us not just what happened but also what always happens. God has been pursuing you and calling out to you, and He is inviting you to be honest about who and where you are so that He can change those things. This is grace upon grace to Cain and those of us who follow in his footsteps.

Is the story of Cain and Abel historically true? Jesus says it is in Matthew 23:35: "…all the righteous blood shed on earth, from the blood of righteous Abel to the blood of Zechariah the son of Barachiah…"

Abel is a picture of a true victim. The Bible says nothing of what he did to instigate or cause this kind of murderous spirit to rise up in his brother. Sometimes you're like Abel—someone is attacking you, and you didn't deserve it. Someone is against you, and you didn't instigate it. Someone is trying to hurt you, and it's not because you hurt them. However, you can't look at every conflict with other people and immediately label it as their fault. If you're going to be Abel, you need to be willing to accept the fact that sometimes you're Cain.

One of the 10 Commandments is "You shall not murder."[a]

[a] Exodus 20:13

It's not just killing—murder is the taking of an innocent life. Jesus takes it a step further in Matthew 5:21–22: "You have heard that it was said to those of old, 'You shall not murder...' But I say to you that everyone who is angry with his brother will be liable to judgment..." Jesus says there are two kinds of murder: murder of the hands and murder of the heart. And God sees both.

Where is your heart? There are different ways that we murder people. We murder their reputation, their business, or their family. We speak curses over them, and we hold bitterness toward them. If there is murder in our heart, eventually it'll come out with our words, and sometimes it even comes out with our hands.

Abel is presented as an incredible man of great faith. However, he still got murdered. In the eyes of those without faith, it might appear that his faith failed him. In the same way, there are godly people with strong faith who die of cancer without getting healed, miscarry an unborn child they love and pleaded in prayer to live, and have their spouse walk out despite years of loving marriage. Abel's faith reveals that our reward often does not come in this life but rather in the life to come.

<u>Our Faithful God</u>

Whether Cain was repentant or unrepentant, here's what we know about God: He marks Cain and says, "You're mine." God does that for the believer today with the Holy Spirit, the mark of God's people. In addition, God uses Cain's evil sin for good. Despite this horrifying sin of murder, Abel's death sparks a revival. Genesis 4:26 says, "At that time people began to call on the name of the Lord." Abel is a foreshadowing of the coming of Jesus Christ as the greater Abel whose death has sparked a global revival ever since.

The Bible is ultimately all about Jesus. Until we recognize that Jesus is the center, hero, and theme of Scripture, it is not well understood. And here's the big idea: Jesus is Abel, and we are Cain. Jesus is the better Abel, and we are Cain. Hebrews 12:22, 24 says, "But you have come to...Jesus, the mediator of a new covenant, and to the sprinkled blood that speaks a better word than the blood of Abel."

As you study, it's helpful to see the parallels in Genesis 4 between our Savior, Jesus Christ, and the story of Cain and Abel.

1. Adam and Eve were kicked out of Eden into the wilderness, where Cain and Abel were born. Jesus left Eden to be born in the wilderness of earth.
2. God came as our big Brother, Jesus Christ. Jesus was innocent, like Abel, and we killed Him, like Cain.
3. Cain was the firstborn in all creation. Jesus is the firstborn over all creation.
4. Cain and Abel were sons of Adam. Jesus is the Son of God.
5. Cain and Abel were in God's presence. Because of Jesus, God put His presence in us.
6. Cain was the unrighteous brother of the righteous Abel. We are the unrighteous brother of the righteous Jesus.
7. Cain and Abel gave their sacrifice to God. Jesus is God sacrificing Himself for us.
8. Cain killed the innocent Abel. We killed the innocent Jesus.
9. Abel's death was the first human death. Jesus' Resurrection was the first human defeat of death.
10. Abel's blood cried out from the ground for justice. Jesus rose from the bloody ground to bring justice.
11. Sin conquered Cain. Jesus conquered sin.
12. Cain was marked by God as His possession. Because of Jesus, the Holy Spirit marks us as God's possession.
13. In the days of Cain, people started calling on the name of the Lord. Today, we know that Jesus Christ is the name of the Lord.
14. Cain built the first city named Enoch. Jesus is building the last city named the New Jerusalem.

Dig Deeper.
1. To learn more about Cain and Abel, read Genesis 4.
2. To learn more about Cain's heart problem, read 1 John 3:11-24.

Walk it out. Talk it out.
1. What most surprises you about Cain's failure? Why?
2. What most surprises you about Abel's faith? Why?
3. How is Cain representative of the world while Abel is representative of the Church?
4. How can group members be praying for each other this week?

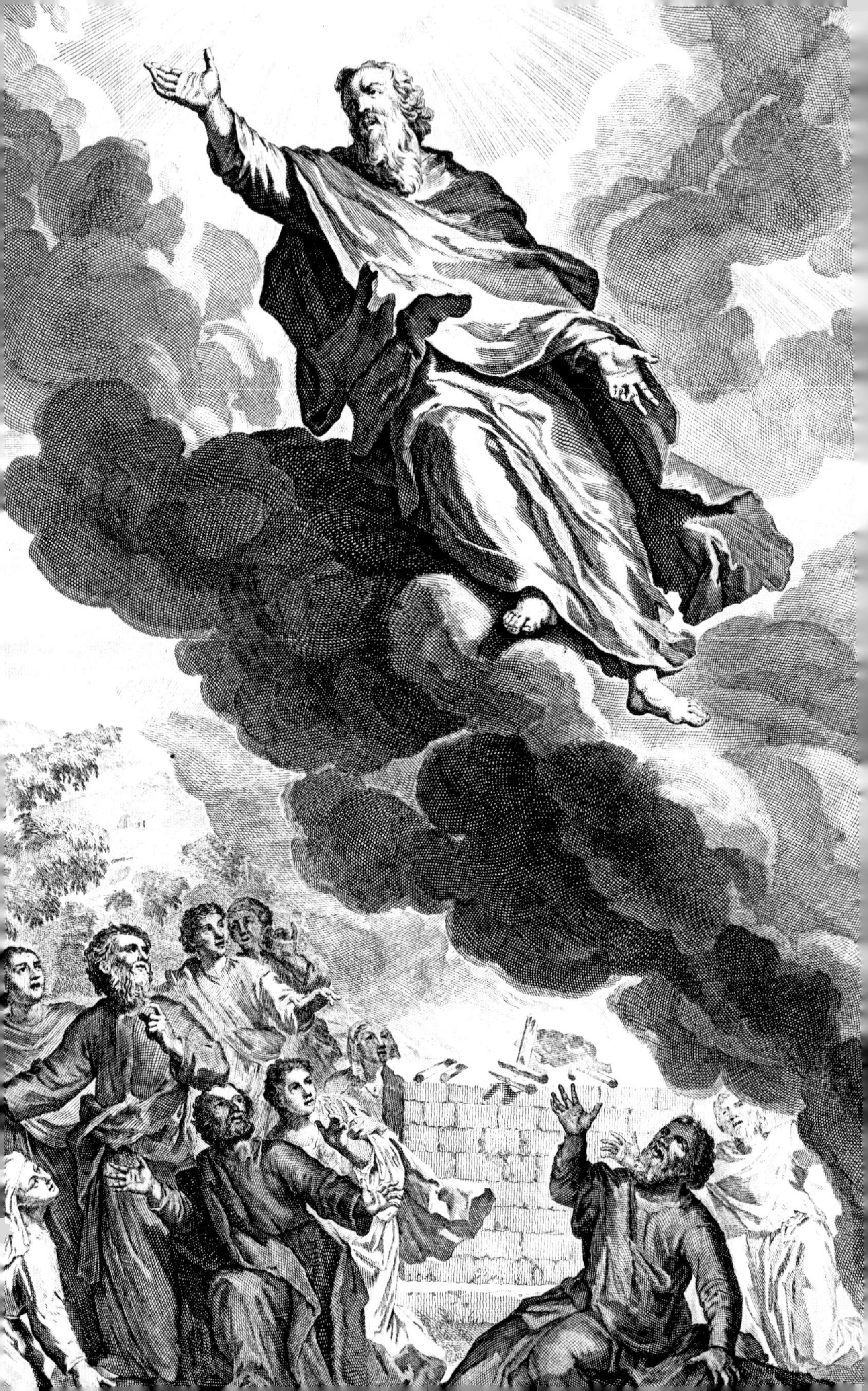

ENOCH

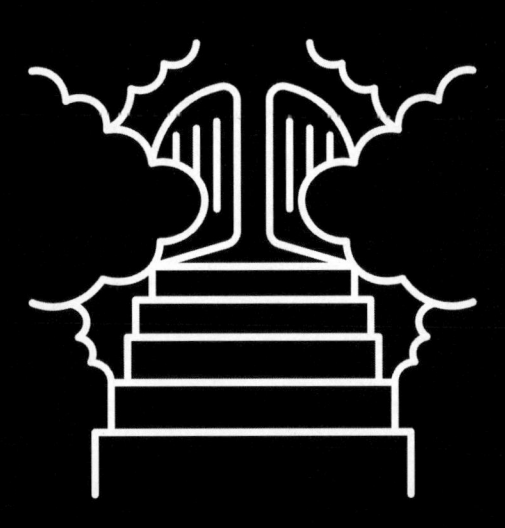

Chapter 3: Faith for Enoch
Hebrews 11:5-6

Hebrews 11:5-6 – By faith Enoch was taken up so that he should not see death, and he was not found, because God had taken him. Now before he was taken he was commended as having pleased God. And without faith it is impossible to please him, for whoever would draw near to God must believe that he exists and that he rewards those who seek him.

With the death of Abel and only the murderous Cain alive to continue the human race (Genesis 4), the question of whether there would be anyone godly on the earth was uncertain. It's against this backdrop that the Bible reports the genealogy of Adam's descendants to Noah. Generation after generation, it simply says the name of the head of the family in that generation, and then eight different times in Genesis 5, it says "he died." The report is stunningly uninteresting. Nothing very noteworthy is mentioned until the seventh generation from Adam is reported in Genesis 5:18-24:

> When Jared had lived 162 years, he fathered Enoch. Jared lived after he fathered Enoch 800 years and had other sons and daughters. Thus all the days of Jared were 962 years, and he died. When Enoch had lived 65 years, he fathered Methuselah. Enoch walked with God after he fathered Methuselah 300 years and had other sons and daughters. Thus all the days of Enoch were 365 years. Enoch walked with God, and he was not, for God took him.

In the entire list, Enoch is the only man said to walk with, meaning to have faith in, God.

Enoch's Faith

With Enoch, a godly line begins, and he becomes the great-grandfather of Noah. A Bible commentary says,

...one man breaks the pattern. As a glittering jewel in a pile of otherwise rather dull stones, we are told of Enoch. *Enoch walked with God; and he was not, for God took him* (5:24). There is a small remnant of faith; there can be true fellowship with God which breaks the thraldom of death, even though change and decay in all around I see. Enoch's faith was his life.[22]

There are three very unique things about this mysterious man, Enoch.

One, Enoch walked with God. The genealogies in Genesis cover 1,656 years of people living and dying—and mention only one person (Enoch) walking with God. Enoch serves as an inspiring example of faith, showing that we can and should walk with God, even if we stand alone and everyone else around us is walking away from God. Enoch's walk with God means that he faithfully worshiped God throughout his life, living in obedience to the Lord. A Bible commentary says,

> The teaching is that Enoch walked with God for 300 years. This was no casual stroll. It was the walk of a lifetime. Moreover, it was a walk and not a sprint or run. Nearly anyone can sprint for a short time or distance, but no one can do it for long. For the long haul you need to walk, and this is what Enoch did. We need people who will walk with God today. Not flashes-in-the-pan. Nor shooting stars who attract you more by their passing brilliance than by their substance. We need steady, faithful people who know God and are coming to know him better day by day.[23]

To walk with God is very practical. It requires more than knowing about God; it requires actually keeping in step with God, like a child on a walk with a father. Speaking of Enoch's legendary walk with God, a Bible dictionary says, "The writer of Hebrews did not say that Enoch thought about God or speculated about Him. He did not read about God or talk about God and thereby gain His favor. Rather, Enoch believed God and thereby pleased God."²⁴

Two, Enoch was history's first prophet, predicting the coming flood with Noah. He was a man of God who preached against all the ungodliness in his day. Enoch preached against sin, as he knew his whole generation was evil, and he said the Lord was coming in judgment with 10,000 angels.[a] Enoch preached about Jesus' Second Coming long before His first coming, by the supernatural revelation of the Holy Spirit. Jude 14-15 says of Enoch,

> It was also about these that Enoch, the seventh from Adam, prophesied, saying, "Behold, the Lord comes with ten thousands of his holy ones, to execute judgment on all and to convict all the ungodly of all their deeds of ungodliness that they have committed in such an ungodly way, and of all the harsh things that ungodly sinners have spoken against him."

Three, Enoch did not die. Enoch is the only man in the genealogy of Genesis 5 that did not die but was spared death. God was so pleased with this man that He rescued him from a corrupt world and brought him Home!

Enoch lived long before the Bible as we have it was written. Enoch had far less information than we do but far greater faith. We have already seen Jesus come the first time, live without sin, die for our sin, and rise to conquer sin and death. We have the completion of the Old and the New Testament. The question is not just how much you believe, but how much you trust that belief. Enoch knew less, but he trusted more. This is why Hebrews 11 presents Enoch as an extraordinary example of faith.

In Enoch, we learn that it doesn't matter how many days you live but rather how many steps you take with God. Enoch did not live to be an old man, but every day, he took another faith step in his walk with God. Nothing else is said about Enoch other than that God was faithful to the man who walked

---

[a] Jude 14-15

out his faith in Him. As a result, Hebrews 11:5 says he "pleased God." This is a remarkable goal for every believer to aspire to by faith—walking with God and pleasing God. This is the simple answer to all sin.

Enoch's Failure

We know so very little about Enoch that no sketch of his life can be made. Other than being a preacher who walked with God and was taken to Heaven before dying, the Bible has nothing more to say.

However, the lack of detailed information about Enoch has caused a great deal of wild speculation. There are books outside the Bible that reference Enoch including "*Jubilees* 4:13–33 and…the Wisdom of Ben Sira (Sirach 47:16) and the Wisdom of Solomon (Wisdom 4:11), both of which suggest Enoch's righteousness."[25]

During the period between the writing of the Old Testament and New Testament, there were books written called the "intertestamental writings" (200 B.C.-A.D. 50). Other books that pretended to be Scripture were also written at later times. These books do contain some helpful historical information along with some wild extra-biblical speculation.

These kinds of books are commonly referred to as the "pseudepigrapha," which in Latin means "wrongly" or "falsely attributed." These are "a group of early writings not included in the biblical canon or the Apocrypha, some of which were falsely ascribed to biblical characters."[26]

These books purport to be written by people in the Bible, which is impossible because they were no longer alive on the earth when they were written. A Bible dictionary reports that these books include:

- The Ethiopic Book of Enoch (*1 Enoch*) may be one of the first apocalypses written.
- The Slavonic Secrets of Enoch (*2 Enoch*) likely dates to the first century AD.
- The Hebrew Book of Enoch (*3 Enoch*) was most likely

written by a Rabbi named Ishmael in the sixth or seventh century AD.[27]

Another Bible resource says,

> A very popular book of the second century BCE was the Book of Enoch, a book of prophecy attributed to him. The acceptance of the book was based on the belief that Enoch, because of his righteousness, was bodily assumed into heaven, and the book was well known to the Jews and early Christians. The author of the letter of Jude quoted a passage from it (Jude 14).[28]

As a mysterious yet godly figure, Enoch has remained popular and the source of many fanciful stories about his life that are not grounded in historical facts. A Bible dictionary says, "In Jewish tradition many fabulous legends gathered around Enoch. He was represented as the inventor of letters, arithmetic, and astronomy, and as the first author. A book containing his visions and prophecies was said to have been preserved by Noah in the ark, and handed down through successive generations."[29]

Our Faithful God

Enoch's relationship with God is noteworthy for two reasons.

First, God was willing to continually walk with Enoch. Like a father walking with a beloved child, what made possible Enoch's walk with God was God's willingness to walk with him. This imagery of a "walk with God" is found throughout the Bible. The first report of God trying to walk with people was Adam and Eve, who hid from God after sinning.[a] A few chapters later, Noah also walked with God.[b] After the Exodus deliverance, God promised to walk with the people and be their God.[c] Sometimes walking with God is referred to as walking

---

[a] Genesis 3:8 [b] Genesis 6:9 [c] Leviticus 26:12, quoted in 2 Corinthians 6:16

before God, as was the case with Abraham[a] and David along with the other kings.[b]

In the days of Jesus, His disciples and followers literally walked with Him wherever He went. The book of Acts reports that the first Christians were called followers of "the Way,"[c] as Jesus said He was "the way,"[d] and they were walking in His footsteps. Speaking of walking with God in the New Testament, a Bible dictionary says,

> Believers are not to walk in darkness (1 Jn 1:1–6; 2 Jn 11) but in the light (1 Jn 1:7); they "must walk as Jesus did" (1 Jn 2:6 NIV), in the truth (2 Jn 4; 3 Jn 3–4), in obedience to God's commands and in love (2 Jn 6). In Paul's letters the figurative use of walking is primarily drawn from Paul's extensive practice of it. In keeping with his tendency toward heightened contrasts, Paul portrays the Christian life in terms of contrasting walks: Christians are to walk in newness of life rather than death (Rom 6:4), in good works rather than trespasses and sins (Eph 2:1–2, 10), as children of light instead of darkness (Eph 5:8), with moral self-control rather than in sensuality (Rom 13:13), by faith rather than sight (2 Cor 5:7). Walking is one of the Bible's vivid metaphors for how godly people should live, both positively in terms of what to follow and negatively in warnings about what to avoid.[30]

Secondly, not only did God walk with Enoch, but God also took Enoch to Heaven without tasting death. Genesis 5:24 says of Enoch, "God took him." It was entirely the sovereign work of God that somehow transported Enoch from earth to Heaven. What a stunning moment that had to be—in an instant, moving from this world to the next without tasting death!

There is one other person in the Old Testament who doesn't die, and that is the prophet Elijah, for whom God sent a chariot to take him to Heaven. Today, there are three people

---

[a] Genesis 17:1 [b] 1 Kings 8:25, 9:24; 2 Kings 20:3; 2 Chronicles 6:16, 7:17; Isaiah 38:3
[c] Acts 9:2, 19:23, 24:14 [d] John 14:6

in Heaven with a physical body: Enoch, Elijah, and, of course, Jesus.

Genesis is the book of beginnings, and Revelation is the book of conclusions. In Genesis, we meet Enoch, the man who never died. In Revelation 11:3-12, there are two mighty prophets who are raised up to preach before Jesus returns in the final judgment. They are then murdered. Some people believe these two prophets are Enoch and Elijah. The argument is made that since they didn't die, they'll be sent down to preach, and then they will die before being resurrected. Time will tell if this hypothesis is true or false.

Through Enoch, God interrupted the normal rhythm of mortality. His life, marked by intimate friendship with God, was crowned by entrance into eternal life—not as a reward for merit but as a sign of future hope. He becomes a type of resurrection life, pointing forward to Christ's triumph over death. Enoch serves as a precursor, foreshadowing, and sneak peek to the future day of Jesus' Second Coming. 1 Thessalonians 4:17 says, "Then we who are alive, who are left, will be caught up together with them in the clouds to meet the Lord in the air, and so we will always be with the Lord."

Dig Deeper.

1. To learn more about Enoch, read Genesis 5:22-24 and Jude 14-15.

Walk it out. Talk it out.

1. What most surprised you about Enoch? Why
2. What are you learning about faith in God so far in our study of Hebrews 11?
3. How is Hebrews teaching you that people in the Old Testament and the New Testament had a relationship with God the same way—through faith? Take some time sharing how God is growing the faith of each group member in this season of their life.
4. How can group members be praying for each other this week?

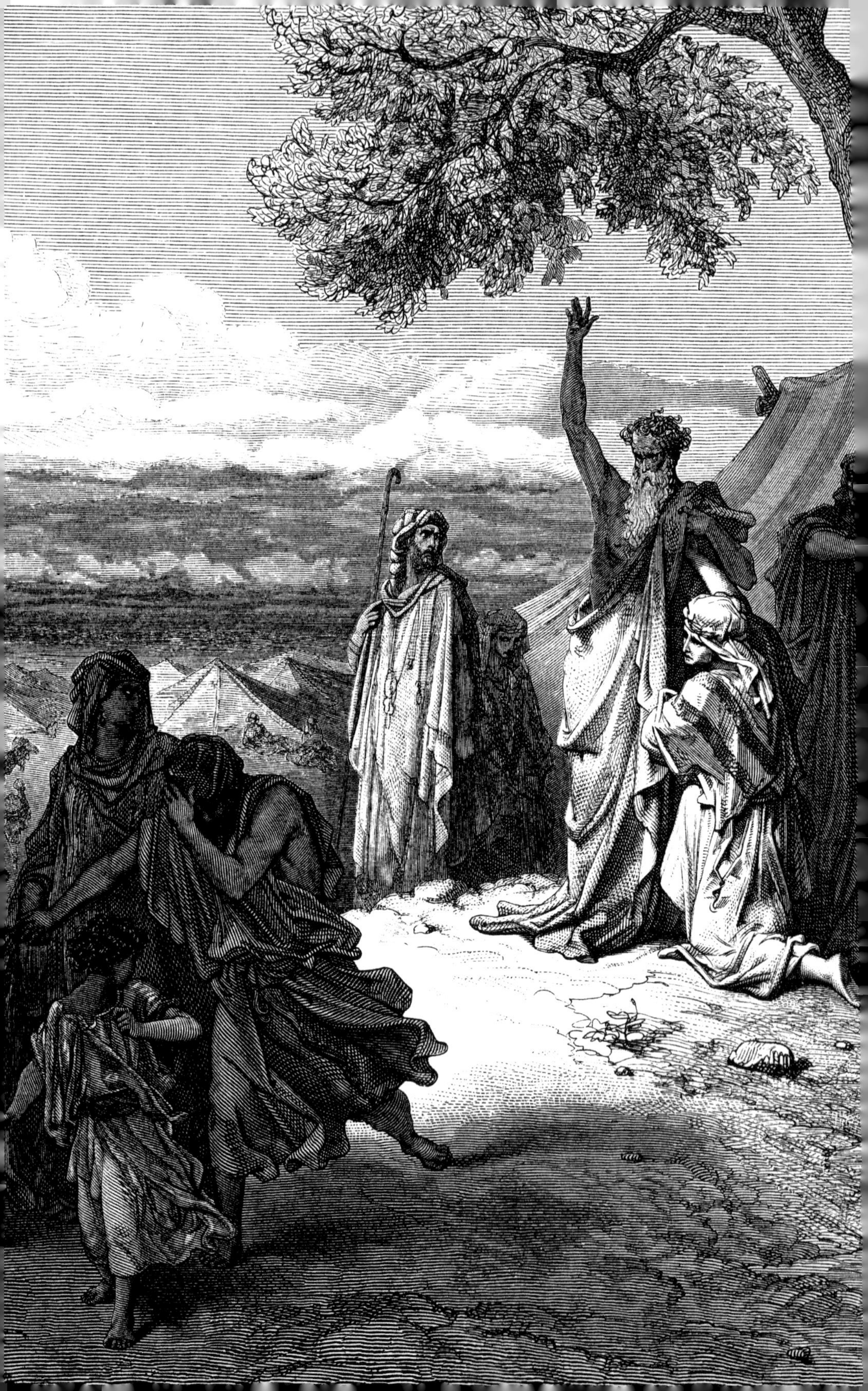

NOAH

Chapter 4: Faith for Noah
Hebrews 11:7

Hebrews 11:7 – By faith Noah, being warned by God concerning events as yet unseen, in reverent fear constructed an ark for the saving of his household. By this he condemned the world and became an heir of the righteousness that comes by faith.

Turning one more page in Genesis from Enoch, we arrive at Noah.[a] The famous story of God calling Noah to build the Ark begins with the lengthy genealogy of Adam's descendants until the birth of Noah. The time span covered in this genealogy is at least 1600 years, and it may be even longer if there are gaps in this genealogy with some generations missing, as there are in other biblical genealogies.[b] The point of the Genesis genealogy is to simply show that every generation and person who descended from Adam were sinners who lived and died without exception in rather monotonous and unspectacular fashion. Genesis 6:3 then says that God would not allow human sin to continue, and therefore He would limit their days to 120 years. 1 Peter 3:20 says, "…because they formerly did not obey, when God's patience waited in the days of Noah, while the Ark was being prepared, in which a few, that is, eight persons, were brought safely through water." If Peter is referring to the 120 years, then God promised His judgment through the flood and then waited patiently for 120 years, providing people an opportunity to repent of their sin, which apparently no one did, and giving Noah time to prepare for the flood and build the Ark. If this interpretation is correct, then Noah also preached during this 120-year period[c], though people were so wicked that they declined God's invitation to forgiveness.

Noah's Faith

Noah obeyed God's commands and built the Ark, likely with only the help of his sons. Hebrews 11:7 says that Noah

---

[a] Genesis 6-9 [b] e.g., compare Genesis 11:31 and Luke 3:36 [c] 1 Peter 2:5

did so in holy fear as a man of faith who believed that God would bring the flood, even while others continued in sin without repentance. Upon completing the construction of the Ark, Noah placed his family on it with the animals God had commanded him to and waited for God to fulfill His promise of judgment in an act of complete faith. The rain continued for 40 days until it covered the land, drowning all of the sinners under God's righteous judgment. The only people spared in the flood were Noah and his family because of God's grace and their faith.

After the flood subsided and God dried the ground, Noah and his family exited the Ark. Then, Noah did a remarkable thing. In Genesis 8:20, we read, "Then Noah built an altar to the Lord and took some of every clean animal and some of every clean bird and offered burnt offerings on the altar."

After recognizing the devastation that God wrought upon the earth, Noah was convicted of his own sin, knowing that he too should have been killed like everyone else. This was not a command from God but rather an act of worship out of Noah's own heart. So, he offered a burnt offering for the atonement of his sin.[a] God was so pleased with Noah's offering of atonement that He responded by promising to never flood the earth again, as the answer to sin would henceforth be atonement, which foreshadowed the death of Jesus for sin.

Throughout the Old Testament, covenant love is God's lovingkindness—the consistent, ever-faithful, relentless, constantly pursuing, lavish, extravagant, unrestrained, one-way love of God. It is often translated as covenant love, lovingkindness, mercy, steadfast love, loyal love, devotion, commitment, or reliability.

God entered a covenant with Noah in Genesis 9:1-17 that was intended for all people of the earth. God promised that He would never again send a cataclysmic flood and that the seasons would continue due to God's provision. In this covenant, we see that God's answer to human sin would be a covenant of grace, beginning with Noah. The sign of the covenant was the

---

[a] E.g., Leviticus 1:4; Job 1:5

rainbow, which served to remind God's people of His promise to never flood the earth again; it may have also symbolized an ancient warrior who hung up his bow after a war as a sign of peace. Tragically, this rainbow symbol has been hijacked by the culture to mock God and celebrate human sin. Through the covenant, God would restore His intentions to bless people as they are commanded to be fruitful and multiply.[a]

One thing noteworthy in the story of Noah is that everyone died—except his family. His wife and sons followed in the footsteps of his faith, enduring mockery and scorn while they built a large boat in the middle of a desert. For men in particular, this fact is worth remembering. Even if your life and witness are rejected by everyone around you, if your family is following you in faith, then you are richly blessed. Ministry begins with your family.

Noah's Failure

After the floodwaters subsided, and Noah's family exited the Ark, his response to God was surprising. In Genesis 9:18-28, Noah responded to God's kindness by getting drunk and passing out naked in his tent like a hillbilly redneck on vacation. Noah's son Ham then walked into Noah's tent to gaze upon his father's nakedness. The Scriptures simply do not tell us much more than these bare details, but many people have inserted numerous scandalous speculations. Whatever happened, one thing is sure: it was sinful and shameful.

In the story of Noah, we have a sort of second Fall with God starting over with Noah, who, like Adam, sinned, along with his son as a sort of second Cain. The point is simply that sin remains the human problem for everyone, even after the flood, which sets the stage for Jesus Christ coming down to save sinners.

---

[a] Genesis 1:28, 5:2, 9:1

HEBREWS 11

Our Faithful God

Genesis 6:5–8 says,

The Lord saw that the wickedness of man was great in the earth, and that every intention of the thoughts of his heart was only evil continually. And the Lord regretted that he had made man on the earth, and it grieved him to his heart. So the Lord said, "I will blot out man whom I have created from the face of the land, man and animals and creeping things and birds of the heavens, for I am sorry that I have made them." But Noah found favor in the eyes of the Lord.

Tragically, the story of Noah is often wrongly told that, in the days of Noah, all the men were wicked except for Noah, who was a righteous man that God saved from His judgment in the flood. The application of this telling of Noah's story is that there are good people and bad people and that God loves and saves the good guys but kills the bad guys, so we should be good guys so that God will love and save us. This false teaching about Noah is simply not what Genesis 6 says and is antithetical to the rest of Scripture that teaches we are saved by God's grace, not because of our good works.

These Scriptures reveal the total depravity of everyone on the earth with one of the most negative declarations about human sin in all of Scripture. We are told that God saw that every person was only evil all the time. God was grieved that He made mankind because they filled His heart with pain. This statement does include Noah, who was simply one of the sinfully wicked men on the earth who grieved God. Noah did not begin as a righteous man but, rather, he began as a sinner as wicked as anyone else on the earth in his day. The only difference between Noah and the other sinners who died in the flood of judgment was that God gave grace to Noah. Beautifully, the word favor is the Hebrew word for grace, which appears here for the first time in the Bible and is echoed repeatedly by Paul throughout the New Testament in his teaching on salvation by grace through faith alone. Because everyone was a sinner in Noah's day, just like everyone is a sinner in our day, God had no good person to work through to accomplish His plan of redemption. So, God worked, as He always has, by saving an undeserving sinner through grace, thereby enabling them to live a righteous life by grace. The order is incredibly important—first, God gave Noah grace, and then, as a result, Noah became righteous and walked with God by grace. As Genesis 6:8-9 reports, "But Noah found favor [grace] in the eyes of the Lord. These are the generations of Noah. Noah was a righteous man, blameless in his generation. Noah walked with God."

Noah was a blameless and righteous man who, like Enoch, "walked with God." But Noah was only this sort of man because God saved him, by grace, and empowered him to live a new life of obedience to God by that same grace. Once made a believer by God's grace, God began to speak directly to Noah and give him commands to obey.

Genesis doesn't tell us just what happened but also what always happens. The Bible is not an old book—it's an eternal book. Because it is timeless, it is always timely. There are two prophecies in the New Testament that tell us how Noah relates to the future of the human race. 2 Peter 3:3-7 says,

> …knowing this first of all, that scoffers will come in the last days with scoffing, following their own sinful desires. They will say, "Where is the promise of his coming? For ever since the fathers fell asleep, all things are continuing as they were from the beginning of creation." For they deliberately overlook this fact, that the heavens existed long ago, and the earth was formed out of water and through water by the word of God, and that by means of these the world that then existed was deluged with water and perished. But by the same word the heavens and earth that now exist are stored up for fire, being kept until the day of judgment and destruction of the ungodly.

Jesus also prophesies about Noah's flood as a foreshadowing

of His final judgment in Matthew 24:37–39:

> For as were the days of Noah, so will be the coming of the Son of Man. For as in those days before the flood they were eating and drinking, marrying and giving in marriage, until the day when Noah entered the ark, and they were unaware until the flood came and swept them all away, so will be the coming of the Son of Man.

God waited patiently in the days of Noah for 1,656 years, and since the Resurrection and Ascension of Jesus, He's been waiting even longer than that. The first judgment was a flood. The second judgment is a fire. God waited patiently to bring the judgment of water, and He's been even more patient until He brings the judgment of fire. Everyone just mocked God until they realized that God was telling the truth. To this day, the scoffers and mockers continue, "being kept until the day of judgment."[a] There is a day coming when God will close the door on human history as he did the doors to the Ark in the days of Noah.

Dig Deeper.
1. To learn more about Noah, read Genesis 6-9.

Walk it out. Talk it out.
1. What most surprises you about Noah's faith and failure? Why?
2. What surprises you about Noah's family and how his wife, sons, and daughters-in-law followed his leadership?
3. What is the most difficult thing God has had you do in obedience to Him?
4. How can group members be praying for each other this week?

---

[a] 2 Peter 3:7

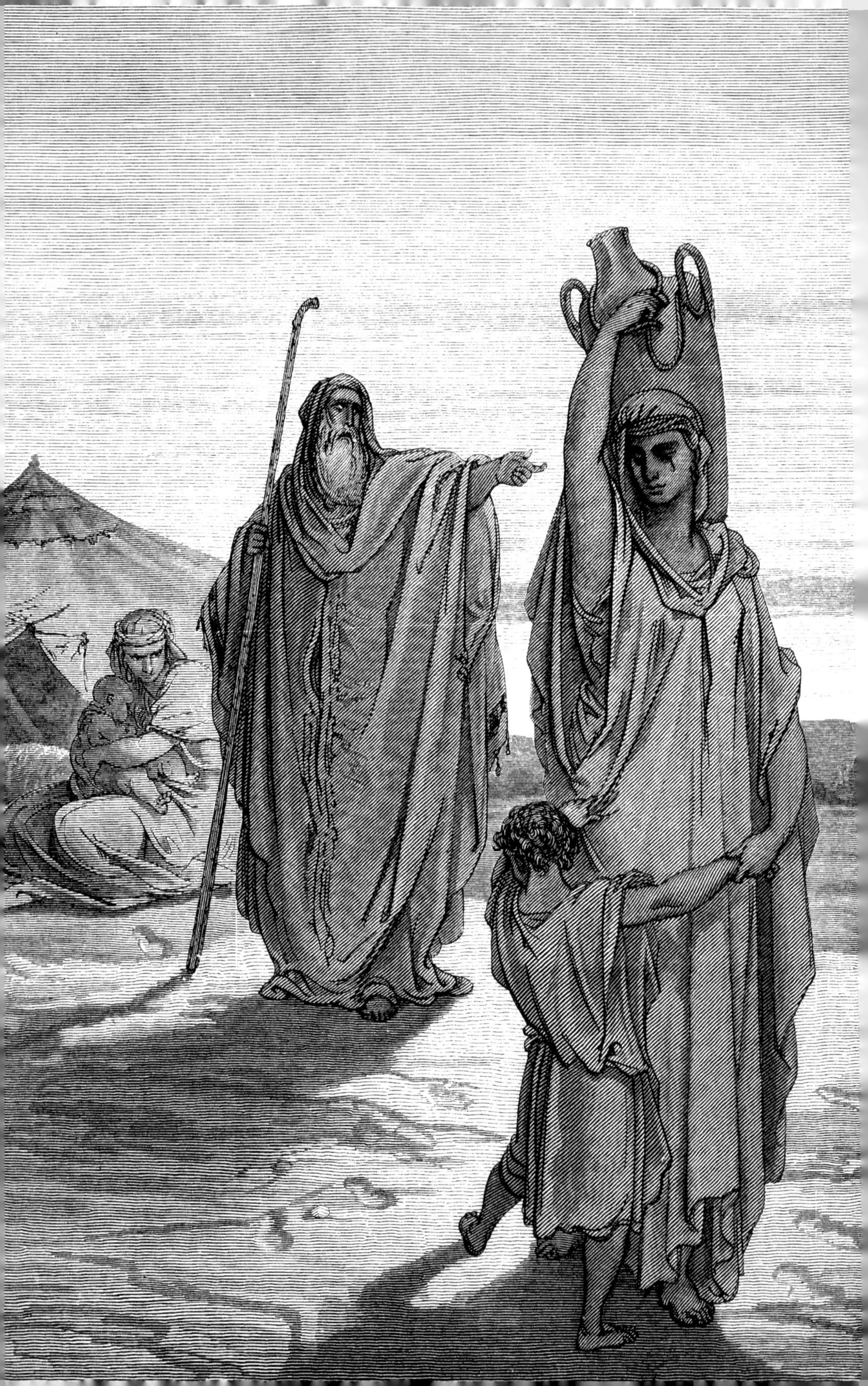

ABRAHAM

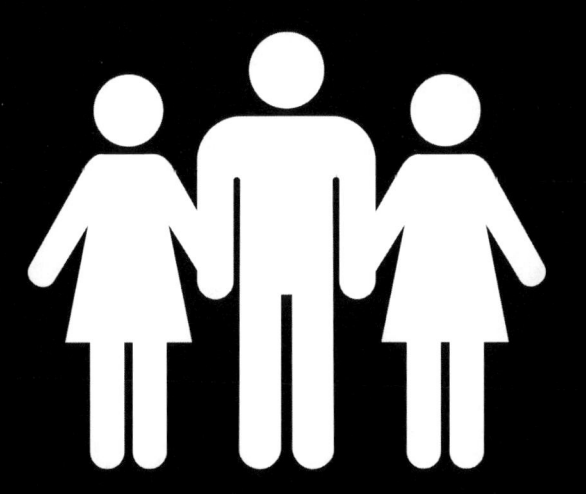

Chapter 5: Faith for Abraham and Sarah
Hebrews 11:8-16

Hebrews 11:8-16 – By faith Abraham obeyed when he was called to go out to a place that he was to receive as an inheritance. And he went out, not knowing where he was going. By faith he went to live in the land of promise, as in a foreign land, living in tents with Isaac and Jacob, heirs with him of the same promise. For he was looking forward to the city that has foundations, whose designer and builder is God. By faith Sarah herself received power to conceive, even when she was past the age, since she considered him faithful who had promised. Therefore from one man, and him as good as dead, were born descendants as many as the stars of heaven and as many as the innumerable grains of sand by the seashore. These all died in faith, not having received the things promised, but having seen them and greeted them from afar, and having acknowledged that they were strangers and exiles on the earth. For people who speak thus make it clear that they are seeking a homeland. If they had been thinking of that land from which they had gone out, they would have had opportunity to return. But as it is, they desire a better country, that is, a heavenly one. Therefore God is not ashamed to be called their God, for he has prepared for them a city.

In human history, some people loom larger than others. One of the most significant men in world history is Abraham, who we meet in Genesis 11, roughly 4000 years ago. Genesis 12-25 goes on to tell the story of him and his wife, Sarah. His name appears over 300 times in the Bible, including 11 books of the New Testament and all four Gospels. In Hebrews 11, as a general rule, each of the "heroes" of our faith is given one verse, but six are reserved for Moses and 12 for Abraham. To this day, three major world religions all look to him as the founder and father of their faith (Jews, Christians, and Muslims).

God had not spoken since His covenant with Noah until He spoke to Abram to initiate a covenant relationship once again. At the time Abram was called by God to become the father of a new nation, the prototype of a life of faith, and one of the most important men in the Bible and human history, he was simply yet another sinner living among the scattered nations. In this way, Abram was not unlike Noah had been before God likewise called him into covenant.

We know very little about Abram before God called him apart from his genealogy, barren wife, and temporary home in Haran after having been born in Ur of the Chaldeans.[a] Since Nehemiah 9:7 and Acts 7:2-3 seem to indicate that God called Abram in Ur of the Chaldeans, he may have even been called out of Babylon and perhaps even sought to help build that great city that God judged in Genesis 11, as the key city of the Chaldeans was Babylon.[b]

Abraham and Sarah's Faith

Amazingly, Abram was apparently just a regular, godless Babylonian when, much like Noah, he, too, found gracious favor in the eyes of the Lord. Amidst God's judging of the Babylonians by scattering them into various nations, God raises up one of their own to conversely be the man through whom God's blessing will be sent forth to the nations. God simply told Abram to leave his homeland and father to journey to a new land that God would show him. God then promised Abram that, though his wife was barren and elderly, he would be a father. Through Abram's son was promised a great nation, blessed by God, that would be a blessing to the nations of the earth through one of his offspring/seed. This promised seed is singular, meaning Jesus, and not plural, meaning Israel.[c] Abram was also told that his descendants would receive the Promised Land if he, in faith, made a radical break with his past.

In faith, Abram believed and obeyed God, doing as God commanded at the age of 75. He took his wife Sarai, their household, and his nephew Lot, who becomes a troublesome figure later in the story. God then appeared to Abram, who responded, in faith, by building an altar to worship God, a

[a] Genesis 11:27-32 [b] e.g., Isaiah 13:19, 48:14; Jeremiah 24:5, 25:12, 50:1; Ezekiel 1:3, 12:13, 23:15 [c] Genesis 3:15; Matthew 1:1, 17; Galatians 3:16

practice he does throughout the book after encountering God.[a] Abram then settled in Bethel, just north of Jerusalem, which is an important city in the Old Testament mentioned more times than any other city but Jerusalem.

The central point of the account of Abram is discovered when contrasting Abram with Babylon, both the story that preceded his call and the city that he was called from. The Babylonians sought to be a great nation, blessed people, great in name, protected from their enemies, and the centerpiece of world affairs. But they pursued their aims apart from faith and God. So, God called one of them, Abram, out into covenant with Himself and promised to give to Abram, by His gracious provision, all that the Babylonians had strived for. Therefore, God is showing that our hope cannot rest in the efforts of sinners to save and bless themselves. Rather, our only hope is to be found by entering into a covenant relationship with God by faith.

Abraham and Sarah's Failure

Abraham's story begins by entering Egypt to escape a great famine.[b] He feared that men would so desire his beautiful wife that she should lie and say that she was his sister so that he would not be harmed. The unsuspecting Egyptians believed Abram's lie, bringing the lovely Sarai to the great Pharaoh and rewarding Abram with gifts for the right to pursue his wife, whom they thought was his sister. Oddly, Pharaoh, who is the godless man in the story, appears more morally upright than the godly man Abram. However, God punished Pharaoh until the secret was revealed, and Sarai was released to Abram. By God's grace, she had not yet been sexually violated.

Abram and his closest relative, Lot, became so prosperous (showing the fulfillment of God's promise to bless Abram and that others would be blessed by him) that they needed to separate because the land could not accommodate both of their households and animals. Abram allowed Lot to select

[a] Genesis 12:7, 8; 13:18; 22:9 [b] Genesis 12

which portion of land he would choose. Thankfully, Lot did not choose the Promised Land, and God made good on His promises in spite of His servant.

After nearly giving away both the Promised Land and his wife, Abram called on the name of the Lord in worship[a], which refocused his faith back to God after a time of repentance. Since he did so at the place where his faith began, it is likely that Abram's return to this place was also his return to trusting God by faith. While God's servants are imperfect, it is His sovereign protection that saves us from ourselves and makes His promises become reality. The point is clear: even when we are faithless, our God remains faithful.

God's dealings with Adam, Noah, and Abraham in Genesis reveal a pattern of God speaking to them, calling them into covenant, establishing them as the head of a new humanity, promising to bless them, and inviting the men to respond to Him in faith. We then see each man falter in faith and sin against the Lord, despite His patient kindness to them.

In Genesis 15, God makes a covenant with Abram, promising him the land of Israel and the lineage of the Hebrews, from whom Jesus Christ would come. Just one chapter later, we see another mini-Fall as, instead of two trees, one of which is forbidden, we now have two women, one of whom is forbidden. Abram's wife, Sarai, had been promised a son in chapter 15, but as she continued to age, 10-plus years had passed since this promise, and their faith faltered. She encouraged her husband to bear a son with his Egyptian maidservant, Hagar.

Abram practices polygamy, marrying Hagar in addition to Sarai, defying God's intention that each man should have one wife.[b] The results of this polygamy are truly tragic, as is the case with other instances of adultery and polygamy in Scripture, which bring favoritism, fighting, jealousy, and mistreatment.[c] The first man recorded in Scripture to take more than one wife was the godless man, Lamech.[d] In the New Testament, church leaders who serve as the pattern for Christian families are to

[a] Genesis 13:4 [b] Genesis 2:18; Matthew 19:4-6 [c] e.g., Genesis 25:28, 27:1-45, 35:22, 38:18-28; II Samuel 3:2-5, 13:1-29, 15:1-18:33; I Kings 11:1-4 [d] Genesis 4:19-24

be one-woman men.[a] Though he was not married on earth, the Lord Jesus has one bride, the Church, and serves as the perfect example of fidelity to the covenant of marriage.

Abram slept with Hagar, and she bore him a son. And, in bitter irony, Sarai blamed Abram for the rift in their family because he slept with Hagar, despite the fact that she had encouraged him to do so. Much like Adam, Abram was passive, allowing Sarai to send Hagar away into the desert. Moses, the author of Genesis, carefully paints this picture in harsh terms, showing the mistreated Hagar sitting alone and heartbroken near a spring in the desert.

Anyone who is married will tell you how easy it is to fall into negative routines and old ruts, even though it always makes things worse and never better. In the marriage of Abraham and Sarah, we see this principle playing out painfully. In Genesis 20:1-18, we read of the account of Abraham moving and, once again, giving away his wife, now around 90 years of age, as he had previously in Genesis 12:10-20. Fortunately, God intervened through a dream that revealed to King Abimelech of Gerar that Sarah was, in fact, married and that God was going to kill him and his family if he touched her sexually. Moses tells the story in such a way as to stress the innocence of Abimelech.[b] It is also, once again, clear that Abraham is a coward and that Sarah joins him in a lie. The story shows that, sometimes, sadly, there are people who do not know God that behave better than the people who do know God.

In Genesis 20:7, God declares that Abraham is a prophet. Until this point, God has been the one functioning like a prophet, calling creation into existence by His Word and speaking to His people directly but not really speaking through His people. God uses Abraham's sin to evangelize Abimelech, telling Abimelech that Abraham will pray for him and that those prayers will be answered. Since we've all had moments like Abraham, it's an encouragement that God can take our mess and turn it into our ministry.

Abimelech, who has been tricked and lied to, asks Abraham

---

[a] 1 Timothy 3:2,12 [b] e.g., Genesis 20:6

why he lied and put him in harm's way with God. Abraham answered that he feared that Abimelech might harm him to take Sarah, and so he sought to protect himself in unbelief rather than trusting God to protect him, as God had promised and demonstrated previously. In a selfish admission, when it came down to the suffering of himself or his wife, Abraham was willing to cause his wife harm to avoid his own. Abraham then tried to weasel his way out of an embarrassing situation by telling a lame, half-truth excuse for sin instead of simply repenting.

Amazingly, Abimelech was a kind man, as he blessed Abraham, giving him sheep, cattle, and slaves. He also invited Abraham to live wherever he pleased on Abimelech's vast land. To top it off, Abimelech also gave Abraham 1,000 shekels of silver, which is around 25 pounds. At this point in the story, the godless Abimelech certainly appears as a better man than Abraham, which is more evidence that he was saved by God's grace and not his great works.

Our Faithful God

The Bible is an incredible book for many reasons, including the fact that it shows how God works through people and places to accomplish His will in spite of human folly and sin. The honesty of human shortcomings and greatness of God's grace should give us hope for our lives and the world around us. This is especially seen in Abraham, a man who, thus far, is a nobody in a place that is considered nowhere. He and this place were used by God to change the course of history and reveal to us the character of the One True God.

As we briefly looked at earlier, God's call of Abram in Genesis 15 is one of the most significant chapters in the Bible, one where the vital themes of faith and covenant appear. Genesis opens with God speaking and preparing creation for mankind by the power of His Word. Throughout Genesis, God has thus far spoken to Adam, Noah, and Abram. In Genesis 15:1, God again speaks to Abram in a vision, preparing man for covenant as He had prepared creation for man through the shaping power of His Word. Whereas later in Genesis 20:7[a], Abram is clearly called a prophet, here he is cast in that role as the Word of the Lord had come to him, a phrase repeated some 221 times throughout the Old Testament when God gives His Word to His prophet.

In Genesis 15:2, we also witness the first time that Abram spoke to the Lord in response. Until this point when God spoke to him, Abram simply believed God and obeyed Him. As Abram's faith relationship with God has grown and matured, he now takes the liberty of respectfully inquiring how God will provide for him. Abram's speech may indicate a wavering in his faith, as, when he is silent, it appears Abram acts in faith, and, when he questions God, it appears that doubt is creeping into his mind. If there is doubt, it may be in part because God had already promised Abram a son earlier[b], and some 25 years would pass between God's promise of a son and the birth of that son, Isaac. Since the name Abram means "exalted father," it could have meant that every day of his adult life was painful, as he and his wife were unable to have a son, which could have caused his faith in God's promise of a son to waver, as real faith is rarely perfect faith.

Regarding Abram, later renamed Abraham, Romans 4:18 says, "In hope he believed against hope…" When you believe the possible is possible, that is hope. When you believe the impossible is possible, that is hope beyond hope. For example, a healthy, young married couple believing they can have a baby is hope, but when Abraham and Sarah, who are barren and old enough to be great-grandparents, wait 25 additional years to have a baby, that is hope beyond hope. God poetically promised to be Abram's protector and provider.

God promised that, though Abram was childless and his wife, Sarai, was barren, they would have a son, and through that son a nation of people would be birthed. Genesis 15:6 reports Abram's response to God's Word, which is among the most important verses in the Bible: "And he believed the LORD, and he counted it to him as righteousness." This verse becomes

[a] cf. Psalm 105:8–15 [b] Genesis 12:2

central to the New Testament doctrine of faith and Paul's doctrine of justification by faith.[a] Jesus' brother James also quotes it to show that true faith in God results in good works in life with Him.[b]

God's covenant with Abram was confirmed with a sacrifice and the shedding of blood. The enactment of covenants in the Old Testament is often referred to as the cutting of a covenant, as they are instituted in blood, showing their life-and-death seriousness. All of this foreshadows the New Covenant of our salvation, which was confirmed with Jesus' sacrifice of His own life on the cross and the shedding of His blood.

God then promised Abram that, though his descendants would inherit the Promised Land, it would not be in his lifetime but rather only after a future 400-year exile in Egypt. In this revelation, God foretold the entire account of the 430-year captivity in Egypt recorded in Exodus, which is the next book of the Bible. God then marked out the boundaries of the Promised Land, the nation we know as Israel today.

Thankfully, God intervenes as the hero of both this chapter of Genesis and all the rest of Scripture. Just as God came searching for Adam and Eve in the Garden, the "angel of the Lord" (likely Jesus Himself in a Christophany, where He shows up in history before His birth) came searching for Hagar in the desert. Hagar explained that she was running from the abusive Sarai, and the angel of the Lord told her several things, namely, to return to Sarai and trust that God would protect her like He had Abram. He also tells her several things about her son, including that he would be the father of a great nation, his name would be Ishmael, meaning "God hears" (because God heard her weeping and responded kindly), he would be a "wild donkey of a man," and he would be a hostile warrior towards his brothers, who would descend from Abram.

In this account, the birth of Hagar's son is announced by an angel much like the birth of Jesus is proclaimed by the angel Gabriel in Luke 1. Both announcements are given to the mothers (Hagar and Mary), both women are greeted, both are

---

[a] Romans 4:3; Galatians 3:6 [b] James 2:23-24

told that they will bear a son, both are given God's favor, both are given their son's name, the future achievements of each son are promised, and the women both respond with thanks to God. Ishmael was born to a Hebrew father and Egyptian mother and became the father of the Arab nations that, sadly due to Abram's sin, to this day, are in hostility with Jews and Christians alike, as promised. In this, we see that God does love the Arabs, who today are more likely to be Muslim than Christian, in part because of this great family feud that began with Sarai and Hagar and continues to this day in great wars and conflicts throughout the world, particularly in the Middle East.

In Genesis 17-18, a chapter after Abram's great Fall in having a child with Hagar, God once again solidifies His covenant with Abram. God, once again, spoke to Abram, and Abram, once again, fell on his face in worship to God. God then changed his name from Abram, which means "exalted father," to Abraham, which means "father of a multitude," as the time for God to fulfill His promise of a son for Abram was very near. God then described His covenant with Abraham to include Abraham's descendants.

The terms of God's covenant with Abraham were that he and his descendants would trust God by faith in obedience by walking with God as Enoch and Noah had and that every male of every generation would be circumcised. God then told Abraham that his wife's name would be changed from Sarai, which means "contentious," to Sarah, which means "princess." God also promised that through Sarah would come kings, including the ultimate King of Kings, Jesus Christ, promised to Sarah's great-grandson Judah in Genesis 49:10.

God kindly restated His promise to Abraham that he would have a son, even instructing Abraham to name him Isaac, which means "laughter," as God would get the last laugh. Summarily, God's portion of the covenant to Abraham consisted of offspring[a] and eternal faithfulness.[b] God also kindly answered Abraham's request to bless his other son, Ishmael, even though he was not the son of the promise or covenant. God also

[a] Genesis 17:4-6 [b] Genesis 17:7-8

promised that 12 princes would come from Ishmael in contrast to the 12 tribes of Israel.[a]

In Genesis 18, three men appear to Abraham, and since one is repeatedly called the Lord and Abraham worshiped Him, it was probably Jesus and two angels. The location at which Abraham is visited is the same place he had settled in 13:18, as he had apparently remained in obedience to God who called him to that place. In this, we see a pattern that emerges as God reveals Himself in various miraculous ways throughout Genesis, including speaking (1:3), visions (15:1), and angels (16:7).

God promised Abraham that his descendants would receive the promised land of Israel, grow from a family to a nation, and see Jesus Christ, the blessing to the nations, born through their family line. In giving away the Promised Land once and promised wife twice, Abraham could have ruined God's plan. However, because God is sovereign over us, He saves Abraham and Sarah over and over. God pursues them, speaks to them, and delivers them. Simply, God is faithful to accomplish His promises even when His sinful people complicate His plans through their disobedience. Often, He has to save us from ourselves.

As is the case with the entirety of the Bible, Abraham's faith walk foreshadows the coming of Jesus Christ:

1. God told Abraham to leave his father and home as a picture of Jesus, the Son of God, leaving God the Father and His home in Heaven.
2. God promised Abraham a son who would lead to the coming of Jesus Christ, the Son of God.
3. God promised Abraham his descendant would bless the nations, and Jesus is that blessing.
4. When God promised Abraham numerous spiritual descendants, He was speaking about us who have faith in His God, Jesus Christ!
5. God chose animals to shed their blood and give their lives for the Abrahamic covenant. God chose Jesus

[a] Genesis 25:12-26

Christ, the Lamb of God, to shed His blood and give His life for the New Covenant.
6. Abraham waited by faith in the promise of Jesus' First Coming. We are waiting by faith in the promise of Jesus' Second Coming.

The book of Genesis has been building in anticipation since chapter 12 for the birth of Abraham's promised son, Isaac. In Genesis 21, that hope is realized some 25 long and arduous years later. Abraham's son was born just when and how God promised, and Abraham circumcised his son at eight days of age, just as the Lord had commanded.

Sarah responded with expectedly great joy as the elderly and barren woman was finally holding her baby boy by a miracle of God. Previously, she laughed in mockery of God[a], and now she laughs in worship of God. Her latter joyful response is much like her descendant, Mary, years later at the birth of the promised Son of God, Jesus Christ.

Abraham and Sarah (now 100 and 90 years old, respectively) named the boy Isaac, meaning laughter, just as God had told them. As Isaac grew, tensions again escalated between Sarah and Hagar, who had given birth to Abraham's first son, Ishmael, further showing the pains of polygamy evident throughout Scripture.

The mockery of her young son infuriated Sarah, though it was, in fact, the same kind of laughter she had previously directed at God. Everyone in the storyline of Genesis loves the boy Ishmael (the Lord, the angel, Hagar, and Abraham) except Sarah, who despised him. Nonetheless, God permitted Sarah to send Hagar and Ishmael away and promised Abraham that, though Ishmael was not part of the covenant line that would bring forth Jesus Christ, he would be cared for and protected. In this way, God may not have been discarding Ishmael and Hagar but removing them from an increasingly tense and unpleasant family situation with Sarah.

Abraham sent Hagar and Ishmael out into the desert with

---

[a] Genesis 18:10-15

only some food and a few gallons of water, which is probably all they could carry. Out of water and wandering in the desert with her son, Hagar sat in despair, anticipating that she and her son would die of thirst as the boy wept. In an event similar to the prior events of Genesis 16, "the angel of the Lord" spoke to her. From Heaven, He promised to care for her and her son, make them into a great nation, and provide a well for them to drink from. God remained true to His promise regarding Ishmael, and the boy grew up in the desert as a skilled archer. His marriage to an Egyptian woman is a likely indicator that he did not worship God but lived by his own courage and strength, much like his many Arab descendants to this day who do not worship Jesus Christ but look to Ishmael as their father. Curiously, this region in Saudi Arabia is the birthplace of Mohammed, who is a descendant of Ishmael and father of all Arabs. It is near the Muslim holy site of Mecca, where the pre-incarnate Jesus Christ visited Ishmael and Hagar. This well is also a Muslim holy site called the Zamzam Well.

Having now calmed the tensions in the storyline of Abraham's families with their conflicts resolved, the master storyteller Moses has reserved the climactic test of Abraham's faith for the near sacrifice of Isaac in Genesis 22, which we will study next. However, before examining the life of Isaac, the following list of encouragements from the lives of Abraham and Sarah should help increase your faith in God:

1. If God can forgive and use Abraham, He can forgive and use you.
2. If you've failed your test, God can use it for your testimony like He did for Abraham and Sarah.
3. If you've made a real mess of your life, God can make it into a redemptive message like He did for Abraham and Sarah.
4. If you've lived by sight, God can open your eyes to live by faith like He did for Abraham and Sarah.
5. If you've made some bad financial decisions, God can still bless you as He did Abraham and Sarah.
6. If God can save this marriage, God can save your

marriage.
7. If God can rescue this family, God can rescue your family.
8. If you have gone south, God will help you turn around and go north.
9. If your life gets awful, God will meet you at the altar.

<u>Dig Deeper.</u>
1. To learn more about Abraham and Sarah, read Genesis 12-23.

<u>Walk it out. Talk it out.</u>
1. What most surprises you about Abraham and Sarah's faith? Why?
2. What most surprises you about Abraham and Sarah's failure? Why?
3. What is the biggest warning for you from the story of Abraham and Sarah?
4. How can members of the group be praying for each other this week?

HEBREWS 11

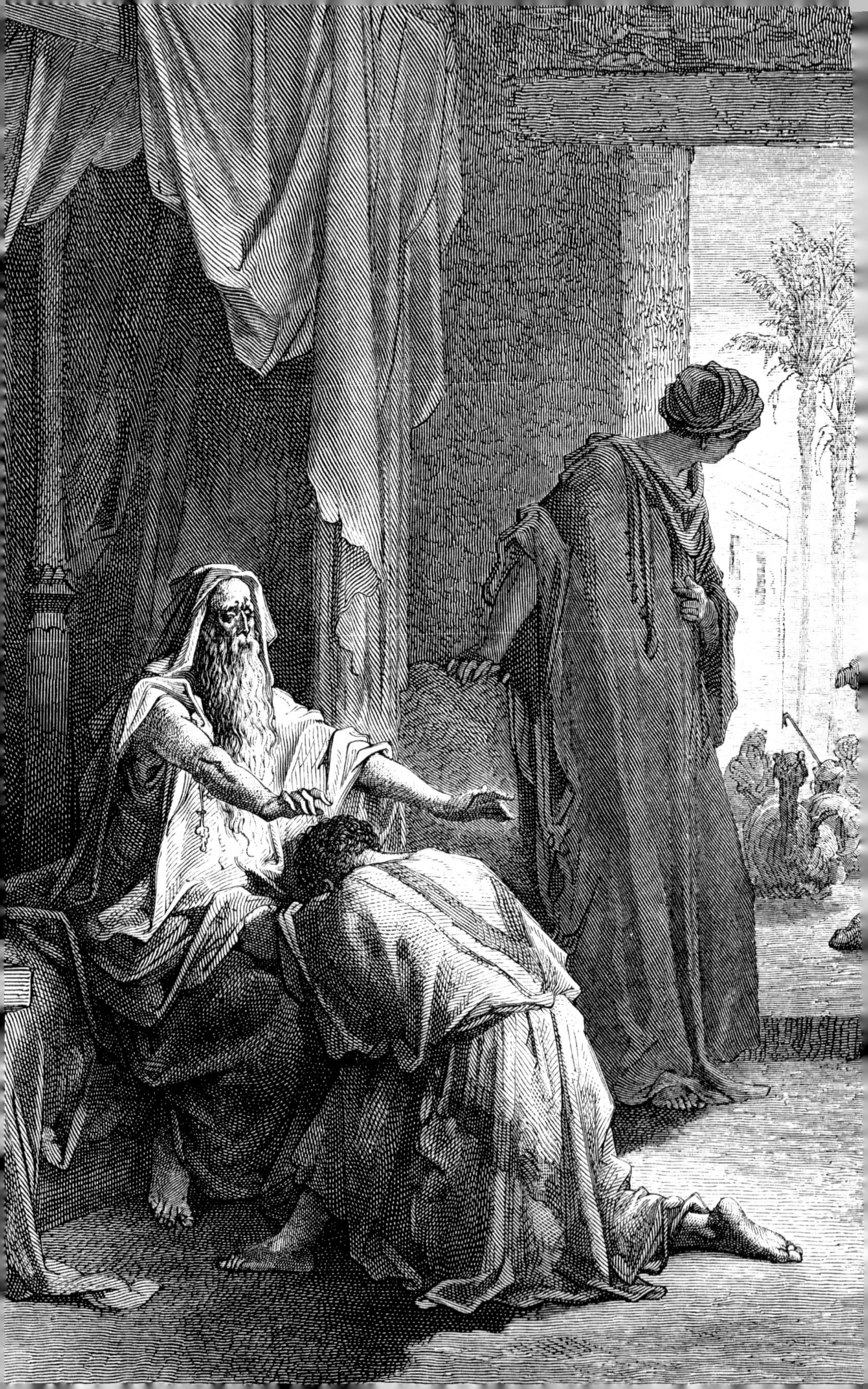

ISAAC

Chapter 6: Faith for Isaac
Hebrews 11:17-20

Hebrews 11:17-20 – By faith Abraham, when he was tested, offered up Isaac, and he who had received the promises was in the act of offering up his only son, of whom it was said, "Through Isaac shall your offspring be named." He considered that God was able even to raise him from the dead, from which, figuratively speaking, he did receive him back. By faith Isaac invoked future blessings on Jacob and Esau.

The adage "the calm before the storm" reminds us that just when it seems life has settled down into a tranquil state, something invariably rolls in like a hurricane. Genesis 21 concludes with the serene portrait that Abraham's life has finally all come together under God's blessing. Despite nearly losing his wife twice, Abraham still has Sarah. Despite waiting for 25 years, Abraham finally has their promised son, Isaac. After residing near the Philistine king Abimelech for some time, the land he had been using, at the kindness of the king, was given to him complete with a well to provide fresh water for his large household. The serene scene ends with Abraham planting a tree as a sign of rest, as it appears the drama and uncertainty of his life has come to an end as he settles down to enjoy his days with his wife and son.

<u>Isaac's Faith</u>

However, Genesis 22 is then a brilliant literary contrast to the portrait at the end of Genesis 21. Sometime later, when Isaac was likely a young man, "God tested Abraham."[a] This statement clues us in that God intends not to lead Abraham into sin but rather to prove Abraham's faith, as our old English word for "test" means. Perhaps the point of this test was not for God to see if Abraham had faith but rather for Abraham to demonstrate the depth of his faith in front of his son Isaac so

---
[a] Genesis 22:1

that he too would learn to walk in faith as his father had. Echoing God's initial call to Abraham in Genesis 12, God commanded Abraham to "go" and sacrifice his son Isaac as a burnt offering. This would have required that Abraham slaughter his son, dismember him, and burn his body. This was later directly forbidden by God.[a] Obediently, Abraham awoke early the next morning without any noticeable hesitation and set out on the roughly 50-mile trek with his son to do as the Lord commanded.

With the knife in the air above him, just before he murdered his son, the angel of the Lord (again, likely Jesus Christ pre-incarnate) called to Abraham from Heaven, commanding him not to harm his son. God then provided a ram to be sacrificed instead. The angel of the Lord again spoke from Heaven, reiterating God's covenant promises to give Abraham blessing, descendants, and land and to bring Jesus through his family as the blessing to all nations of the earth. After having walked with God for many years and seeing Him provide in very difficult situations, Abraham had apparently learned to trust God no matter what. His faith in God was so resolute that he believed that, even if he killed his son, God, who gave him the son through a conception miracle, could give him back through a resurrection miracle.

Today, it's 4,000 years later. We've seen Jesus die, rise, and prove His Resurrection. We remind ourselves every Easter now that we know about the resurrection of the dead, but Abraham did not have this knowledge. Abraham was demonstrating incredible faith in this act of testing.

Let's be honest: Abraham has had some difficult days. His walk with God is two steps forward, one step back. But Genesis 22 reveals mature, seasoned faith; this is tested and proven faith. If Abraham believed that God could bring someone back from the dead, then you and I should believe that God is going to bring us back from the dead. Jesus already proved it, so not only do we have faith, but we also have sight. Furthermore, Isaac's submission to God's command to lay down his life as a

---

[a] Leviticus 18:21, 20:2

younger and stronger man than his elderly father, Abraham, was an act of his great faith in God.

Having fathered a child with a woman who worshiped another god and experiencing the lifelong pain of that sin, Abraham is determined that his son Isaac marry a godly woman. Genesis 23 reports that Abraham sent his servant back to his hometown to find a wife for his son. Abraham trusted that the God who had blessed him in every way would be faithful to now provide a godly wife for Isaac by sending an angel ahead to arrange the details.

Abraham's faithful servant did as he was told and went to the region of Abraham's brother, Nahor. Stopping at a spring, the servant prayed for God to provide. Before he had finished his prayer, God had already answered it, sending the lovely virgin Rebekah to the spring. Rebekah drew water for Nahor and his animals and was clearly a very sweet and kind woman. When the servant inquired of her family, she said her father was Nahor and that he was welcome to stay at their home. The servant was so overjoyed at God's perfect provision that he bowed down and worshiped the Lord for answering his prayer.

Upon arriving at Abraham's household, Rebekah was brought into the former tent of Isaac's mother, Sarah, and she married Isaac. The account of Isaac and Rebekah's marriage ends with the beautiful words that "he loved her," and she was such a delightful woman that he was comforted by her love after the death of his mother. Subsequently, Isaac is now positioned to take the place of Abraham, and Rebekah is positioned to take the place of Sarah in the family and their family ministry.

Despite Abraham's faults, flaws, and failures, God proves faithful. God made a series of promises to Abraham throughout Genesis that are fulfilled by the end of his life:

1. God promised to bless him (12:2)
2. God promised the Promised Land he was buried in (12:7) with Sarah (23:19)
3. God promised a son through Sarah (15:4)
4. God promised that Abraham would live to a good old age (15:15)

5. God promised Abraham that nations would come from him (17:5, 16)
6. God promised Abraham that kings would come from him (17:6, 16)
7. God promised that salvation and faith would continue into future generations (17:7)

With Abraham, his wife Sarah, and his son Ishmael now all dead, Moses moves the Genesis story forward to focus on the birth of Isaac's sons, Jacob and Esau. Isaac was 40 years old when he married Rebekah, and, like Isaac's mother, she was unable to conceive a child. Isaac trusted that God could and would give Rebekah a son just as God had given him to his barren mother, Sarah. Importantly, Isaac remains faithful to his wife, unlike his father, Abraham, so the sin of adultery is not passed on to the next generation. Instead, Isaac prayed in faith for 20 years for the blessing of children, and God answered the prayer, giving the couple twin boys when Isaac was 60 years old.

Curiously, while the other family lines in Genesis are usually quite large, Isaac only has two sons. But, while the 12 sons of Isaac's half-brother Ishmael are mentioned in only a few verses, Isaac's sons Esau and Jacob receive nearly 12 chapters of attention in Genesis (25:19-37:1) because they relate to the promises of the covenant.

Isaac's Failure

Isaac's failures were largely in faith and family. His spiritual life is less robust than his father Abraham's. God speaks to him less, appears to him less, and his family is less spiritually devoted. Furthermore, his son Esau marries godless women. Genesis 26:34-35 says, "When Esau was forty years old, he took Judith the daughter of Beeri the Hittite to be his wife, and Basemath the daughter of Elon the Hittite, and they made life bitter for Isaac and Rebekah."

Though Isaac stays faithful to Rebekah in not taking another wife, in Genesis 26, he falls into the same sin pattern as his father, Abraham. In both cases, there was a famine causing the men to come to the pagan king of a neighboring nation for assistance. Both husbands had beautiful wives and feared that the kings would desire them, so they lied, saying their wife was actually their sister. The goal was to prevent the kings from harming or killing the husbands in order to take their wives.

At the end of his life, the time came for Isaac to pass on the family blessing of the Abrahamic covenant to one of his two sons, Jacob or Esau.[a] God had already spoken of this matter from conception, saying in Genesis 25:23, "And the Lord said…'Two nations are in your womb, and two peoples from within you shall be divided; the one shall be stronger than the other, the older [Esau] shall serve the younger [Jacob].'" Isaac and Rebekah played favorites with their sons, which is a sin that caused repeated family strife in the generations of Genesis. Rebekah favored Jacob, who was a soft, homeward-oriented momma's boy; Isaac favored Esau, who was a tough, warrior-type man's man. Isaac was supposed to pass the generational blessing onto Jacob, in obedience to God, but planned to sin against God and give it to Esau instead. This would have upended God's entire plan for the descendants who would lead to Jesus Christ. The opening lines of Matthew's Gospel make this plain, saying, "The book of the genealogy of Jesus Christ… the son of Abraham. Abraham was the father of Isaac, and Isaac the father of Jacob…" Furthermore, God is repeatedly referenced as the God of "Abraham, Isaac, and Jacob."[b] Rebekah and Jacob devised a plan of deception to take the blessing from Esau and give it to Jacob, showing a dishonest family led by a man who was going to fail in a massive way at the end of his life. In the end, Jacob received the blessing of the Abrahamic Covenant, despite his sin and the sins of his mother and father.

<u>Our Faithful God</u>

What was God doing with the sacrifice of Isaac? He told Abraham to "go to the land of Moriah" and offer Isaac "as a burnt offering on one of the mountains of which I shall tell

---

[a] Genesis 27 [b] Matthew 8:11, 22:32; Mark 12:26; Luke 3:34, 13:28, 20:37; Acts 3:13, 7:32

you."[a] Many years later, God showed up to King David on that very same mountain and told him that his family would build a temple where the Lord would be worshiped in that place. 2 Chronicles 3:1 says, "...Solomon began to build the house of the Lord in Jerusalem on Mount Moriah..." The temple was built in the place where Abraham almost sacrificed Isaac, and it became the place of substitutionary atonement. It's the place where the priest—the mediator between man and God—would take an animal, impute the sins of the people to the animal, and then slaughter it as a substitute.

Hebrews 9:22 says, "...without the shedding of blood there is no forgiveness of sins." The temple was the connecting point between Heaven and earth. It's where the presence of God was. It's where sinners would offer a sacrifice, and a substitute would die so that the sinner could be forgiven by the God whom they had sinned against. Blood literally flowed from the temple.

All of this was to prepare us for the coming of Jesus Christ, "the Lamb of God, who takes away the sin of the world!"[b] John 3:16 says, "For God so loved the world, that he gave his only Son, that whoever believes in him should not perish but have eternal life." Jesus Christ substituted Himself for us. We should die and go to Hell to pay God back for all our sins against Him. But God loved us so much that He would substitute His only Son to die for us and then rise from the dead.

The longing, hope, and faith that Abraham had for his son were fulfilled in God's Son. Jesus did die, and He did rise from the dead. Because of Jesus, you can be forgiven for all your sins. You can be reconciled in relationship with God. You can know that your eternal life with God is secure and that your resurrection is guaranteed if you believe in the Son of God, the Lord Jesus Christ. Romans 8:32 says, "He who did not spare his own Son but gave him up for us all, how will he not also with him graciously give us all things?"

The whole Bible is about Jesus. He is the center of the Bible and human history. Everything points to Him, comes from Him, and is held together by Him. This is also true as we

[a] Genesis 22:2 [b] John 1:29

examine the comparisons between Isaac and Jesus:

1. Isaac and Jesus were both born in accordance with promises given many years before.
2. Isaac and Jesus were both born at God's appointed time after years of waiting.
3. Isaac and Jesus were both born of miracles. (Sarah was barren, and Mary was a virgin.)
4. Isaac and Jesus were both firstborn sons.
5. Isaac and Jesus were both loved by their fathers (Abraham, God the Father).
6. Isaac and Jesus both left their father's home (Beersheba, Heaven).
7. Isaac and Jesus both journeyed three days (Beersheba-Moriah, cross-empty tomb).
8. Isaac and Jesus were both escorted by two men to their sacrifice (two servants, two thieves).
9. Isaac and Jesus were both young men who carried wood upon their backs to their sacrifice.
10. Isaac and Jesus both willingly submitted their lives to their father.
11. Isaac and Jesus were both laid down as an offering for sin.
12. Isaac and Jesus both asked their father a question ("Where is the lamb?", "Why have you forsaken me?").
13. Jesus is the Angel of the Lord who spared Isaac and died as the sacrifice for sin.
14. Isaac was promised that God would provide, and Jesus was that provision.
15. Isaac was raised from death figuratively, and Jesus was raised from death literally.
16. Isaac and Jesus went forth to get their bride (Rebekah, the Church).

Genesis 26:1-5 records the Lord appearing and speaking to Isaac as He had to his father, Abraham. Likewise, God promised to be with Isaac, bless him, and give him descendants and land according to the promises of the Abrahamic covenant. God notes that He blessed Isaac because his father Abraham "obeyed my voice and kept my charge, my commandments, my statutes, and my laws."[a] Though Moses had not yet been born, and the law had not yet been given, Isaac obeyed it by faith as a pattern of someone who had God's laws written on their heart by the Holy Spirit.[b]

God was repeatedly faithful to Isaac, even when Isaac was unfaithful to God. Genesis 26 repeatedly reveals God initiating a relationship with Isaac, speaking to him, and blessing him:

> Now there was a famine in the land...And the LORD appeared to him and said, "...I will be with you and will bless you, for to you and to your offspring I will give all these lands, and I will establish the oath that I swore to Abraham your father. I will multiply your offspring as the stars of heaven and will give to your offspring all these lands. And in your offspring all the nations of the earth shall be blessed..." And Isaac sowed in that land and reaped in the same year a hundredfold. The LORD blessed him, and the man became rich, and gained more and more until he became very wealthy...And the LORD appeared to him... and said, "I am the God of Abraham your father. Fear not, for I am with you and will bless you and multiply your offspring for my servant Abraham's sake." So he built an altar there and called upon the name of the LORD and pitched his tent there...[c]

Even a godless ruler said, "We see plainly that the LORD has been with you...You are now the blessed of the LORD."[d]

The adage "Like father, like son" rings true for Abraham and Isaac, as evidenced in the following points:

1. Both men received God's call and promise
2. Both lived during a period of famine
3. Both men dwelt in Gerar
4. Both men had lovely wives

[a] Genesis 26:5 [b] E.g., Jeremiah 31:33 [c] Genesis 26:1-4, 12-13, 24-25 [d] Genesis 26:28-29

5. Both men were cowards in the face of possible harm
6. Both men lied and said their wife was their sister
7. Both men were spared the consequences of their sin by God's mercy
8. Both men were rebuked by more pious Gentiles for their lying schemes
9. Both men were pursued by Abimelech (Isaac may have actually dealt with Abimelech's son or grandson with the same name) for a covenant
10. Both men were a blessing to their neighbors
11. Both men trusted God and lived peacefully with their neighbors

Today, Isaac is mentioned in 21 books of the Bible, appearing 19 times in the New Testament. With Isaac's life ending, the focus of Genesis then shifts from Isaac to the next generation, with his son Jacob revealing God's faithfulness from generation to generation.

Dig Deeper.
1. To learn more about Isaac, read Genesis 22, 24, and 26.
2. To read Paul's commentary on the life of Isaac, read Romans 9:6-11.

Walk it out. Talk it out.
1. What most surprises you about Isaac and Rebekah's faith and failure? Why?
2. What did the Holy Spirit highlight for you as you studied the near sacrifice of Isaac by his father, Abraham, in Genesis 22?
3. What is the biggest risk and/or sacrifice God has asked you to make?
4. How can group members be praying for one another this week?

HEBREWS 11

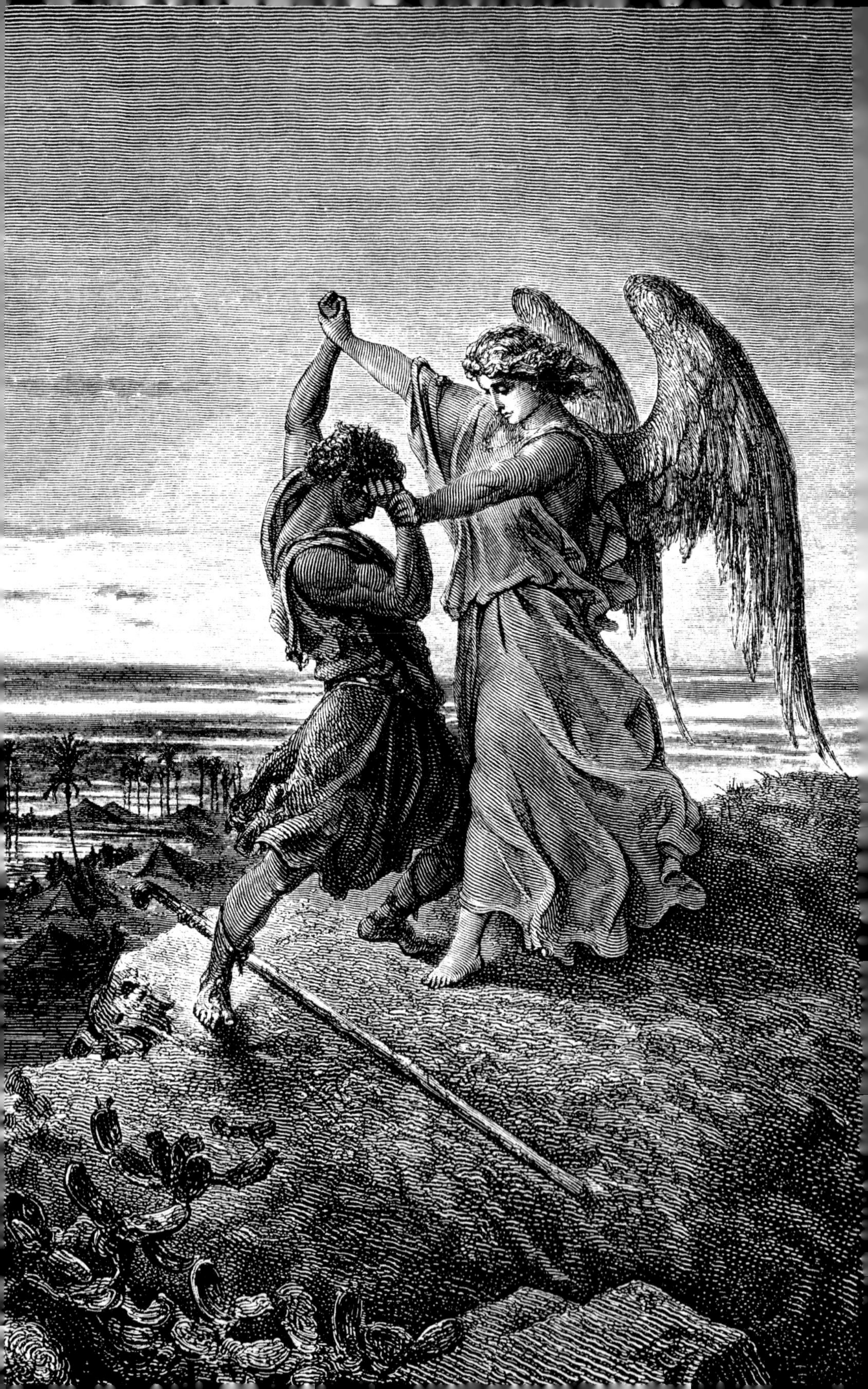

JACOB

Chapter 7: Faith for Jacob
Hebrews 11:21

Hebrews 11:21 – By faith Jacob, when dying, blessed each of the sons of Joseph, bowing in worship over the head of his staff.

Unlike his grandfather, Abraham, who commanded an army and led men into battle, Jacob began as a soft man, needing to be toughened up by life to become a leader used of God. His faith is weak at best, and he is not maturing or growing much as a man of God in his early years.

Genesis 28 takes a significant and dramatic turn when God appears to Jacob at night to bless him with the promises of land, descendants, and blessing for all nations, much like He had his grandfather Abraham in Genesis 15. After God appears, Jacob recognizes Him and names the place where God had met him "Bethel," which means "house of God." For the first time in his life, Jacob has encountered God. Subsequently, this is the beginning of Jacob not living under the faith of his parents but, for the first time, beginning his own relationship with God so that the God of Abraham and Isaac could also be known as the God of Jacob. The turn in Jacob's heart toward God first appears in his declaration that he will tithe to God, which is the first instance of worship we have seen from him thus far and may indicate his conversion.

In Genesis 29-30, Jacob the trickster is tricked into working 14 years for an evil man named Laban to marry the woman of his dreams. He wanted to marry the lovely Rachel, but her dad swapped out his daughter in the dark bridal tent, and Jacob accidentally consummated his marriage with her sister Leah! Jacob hated Leah, who kept having his children, and loved Rachel, who struggled to become a mother. Jacob's family was a complete mess.

At this point in the story, Jacob is now an old man (perhaps in his 80s) with two wives who are sisters. In the ensuing years, the family drama is more intense than any daytime soap opera—complete with multiple adulteries, child births, and a small harem of women manipulating Jacob, who is a believer but very weak in his faith. Through it all, God would preserve His covenant through Jacob's sons, who would become the 12 tribes of Israel, through whom Jesus would be born to deal with the human sin problem that was so evident in Jacob's family. The theme of this section, as with the rest of Genesis and the Bible, is that God is the hero that rescues self-destructive sinners from themselves by His grace and mercy alone.

Jacob's Faith

After 20 years working for his father-in-law Laban, Jacob wanted to return home to his mother, Rebekah, and father, Isaac. In faith, Jacob entrusted himself to God's plan, despite opposition from his evil father-in-law. Jacob rejected Laban's offer to stay and work for him and entrusted himself to the Lord's provision alone. God honored Jacob's faith and made him into a very wealthy man.

God then spoke to Jacob in Genesis 31:3 as he had to his grandfather Abraham in Genesis 12:1, calling him to leave what had been his home for 20 years to return to his family. Jacob responded in faith, for the most part. Jacob left home as a single man and now returns home as a husband and father who has been toughened up by years of abuse under his father-in-law, Laban.

In Genesis 32:9–12, we then see the faith of Jacob, which has apparently been growing slowly over the 20 years since he first encountered God personally, as he prayed to God in faith that God would be faithful to His covenant promises to bless and protect him. Jacob's faith matured over decades of life, and it was not until his mother stopped coddling him and life got challenging that he became a man of growing faith. The lesson is simple: faith grows best under struggles and trials.

Jacob's Failure

After stealing the covenant blessing from his brother Esau, Jacob ran for his life, moving away from his mother and father to live with his father-in-law, Laban, who is more of a conniving trickster than Jacob himself, who deceived his own blind, dying, elderly father. Jacob is a classic late bloomer. He is overmothered, soft, and spoiled. Early in his life, he was coddled by his mother, lived off the wealth and blessings God poured out on his father, Isaac, and schemed to benefit himself, including robbing his own brother. He is incredibly selfish and lacks character until he is an older man, finally growing in courage, fortitude, and faith because God allowed hardship to toughen him up over decades of struggle.

In the next chapter, Hebrews 12:5-11 says,

> And have you forgotten the exhortation that addresses you as sons? "My son, do not regard lightly the discipline of the Lord, nor be weary when reproved by him. For the Lord disciplines the one he loves, and chastises every son whom he receives." It is for discipline that you have to endure. God is treating you as sons. For what son is there whom his father does not discipline? If you are left without discipline, in which all have participated, then you are illegitimate children and not sons. Besides this, we have had earthly fathers who disciplined us and we respected them. Shall we not much more be subject to the Father of spirits and live? For they disciplined us for a short time as it seemed best to them, but he disciplines us for our good, that we may share his holiness. For the moment all discipline seems painful rather than pleasant, but later it yields the peaceful fruit of righteousness to those who have been trained by it.

The life of Jacob is a case study in this principle—that God is a Father who uses hardship to discipline His children, pressuring them to grow in faith and holiness. God does just this, proving Himself a faithful Father to Jacob.

Our Faithful God

God's faithfulness is apparent throughout Jacob's life,

especially when he was returning home to his elderly parents and brother he fled from roughly two decades prior. Before encountering his brother Esau, who wanted to kill him the last time they were together, God again appeared to Jacob in a very significant way.[a] While alone one night, a man who is called "God"—likely Jesus—came to Jacob. Though Jacob was an elderly man, he wrestled with the man all night, unwilling to give up until he was blessed. Jacob started wrestling with his twin brother in their mother's womb, wrestled metaphorically with Laban for years, and now wrestles with God.

At daybreak, the men stopped wrestling, and the man changed Jacob's name (meaning "trickster") to Israel (meaning "wrestles with God and perseveres"). He has now matured from a man who excelled by trickery to a man of faith who trusted God to bless and protect him according to the covenant promises. Israel is mentioned over 1,800 times in the Bible, as this is a significant moment in world history.

Jacob had grown in faith, become a servant of God, and was ready to re-enter the Promised Land as a new man with a new name. This is revealed by his prayer, which is the only recorded prayer of any length in Genesis. The man with whom Israel wrestled touched his hip so that he would limp for the rest of his days. This was a reminder to himself and everyone who saw him that God had been patient with him for many gracious years and had blessed him when he could have justly harmed or killed him at any point. The point of this account is that, throughout his life, Jacob was ultimately not wrestling with Laban or Esau but rather God. The same is true for us. Often, like Jacob, whether we know it or not, our struggles are often with God who has blessing for us if we fight through our battles to get to our blessings.

The reunion between Jacob/Israel and his brother Esau after 20 long years of separation is a beautiful portrait of forgiveness. Esau lovingly embraced his brother, welcoming him home. Jacob blessed his brother with generous gifts that he attributed as provided by God; however, Esau did not need

---

[a] Genesis 32

them because he, too, had become a wealthy man, a fact he did not attribute to God like Jacob/Israel did. Obviously, God had been working at changing the hearts of both men.

Jacob then worshiped God by building an altar at Shechem, the first place that his grandfather Abraham had been visited by God and where Abraham built his own altar.[a] Genesis 33 closes with the wondrous portrait of the transformed Jacob worshiping the God not only of Abraham and Isaac but also now the God of Jacob. And much like the literary flow of the story of his grandfather Abraham, the story of Jacob/Israel appears to have climaxed, as he is now an older man blessed by God and ready to relax in peace. However, his presence in Shechem is an ominous hint at what awaits in the following chapter, because he was supposed to continue on to Bethel as God commanded.

In Genesis 35-36, God again spoke to Jacob to go to Bethel, and, like Abraham before him, he obeyed. To purify his household that was apparently filled with spiritual lethargy, godless idols, and superstitions, Jacob commanded that all false gods and other demonic paraphernalia be removed. In this act, we see the progression of Jacob's faith. After wrestling with God and walking away with a more mature faith in Genesis 32, Jacob then witnessed the effects his weak faith had wrought among his children in Genesis 34. So, Jacob responded by rising to become the spiritual leader in his family before returning home to carry on the legacy of a faithful covenant keeper who obeyed God and raised covenant children who likewise obeyed God. After cleansing his household, Jacob again worshiped God.

God responded to Jacob's faith by appearing to him again. God then blessed him and reiterated that his new name was Israel, though in Genesis 34, he had temporarily fallen back into acting like the old Jacob, gripped by fear and self-preservation when he needed to live confidently by faith. God then reiterated His covenant promises of descendants, land, and blessing. Jacob responded by worshiping God, and we are now seeing a rhythm of regular worship and intimacy with God that had been lacking in his life until this point. His faith has

---

[a] Genesis 12:6-7

greatly matured, as is evidenced by the author, Moses, now calling him "Israel" rather than "Jacob" frequently throughout the rest of Genesis.

As they were heading to Bethlehem, Jacob's beloved wife, Rachel, died giving birth to Jacob's youngest son, Benjamin, who became the last of the 12 sons who would become the 12 tribes of Israel. She died in Ephrath, also called Bethlehem, where Jesus was later born.[a]

Thus far in Genesis, a family history has been traced for 2000 years. With the conclusion of Genesis 36, Moses has now provided a complete, albeit selective, account of the lives of Isaac and his sons Esau and Jacob/Israel. Jacob now, too, had transformed from the young, impetuous trickster to a patriarch of faith like his father and grandfather. Jacob's sons got to meet their grandfather, and then Isaac died at the age of 158. His only two sons, Esau and Jacob, buried him. Moses then focuses on the 12 sons of Jacob, as they are the line of covenant promise, paying particular attention to his second-to-youngest son, Joseph. The remainder of Genesis is, in effect, still focused on Jacob through the life of his son Joseph, who takes center stage with an incredible faith journey.

Dig Deeper.
1. To learn more about Jacob, read Genesis 25:19-34 and chapters 27-33 and 35.

Walk it out. Talk it out.
1. What most surprises you about the faith and failure of Jacob? Why?
2. How has God used difficult life circumstances to discipline, mature, and grow you like He did Jacob?
3. Which characters in the story of Jacob do you most identify with, and why (e.g., Jacob, Leah, Rachel, Laban, or Esau)?
4. How can group members be praying for each other this week?

[a] Ruth 1:2, 4:11; 1 Sam. 17:12

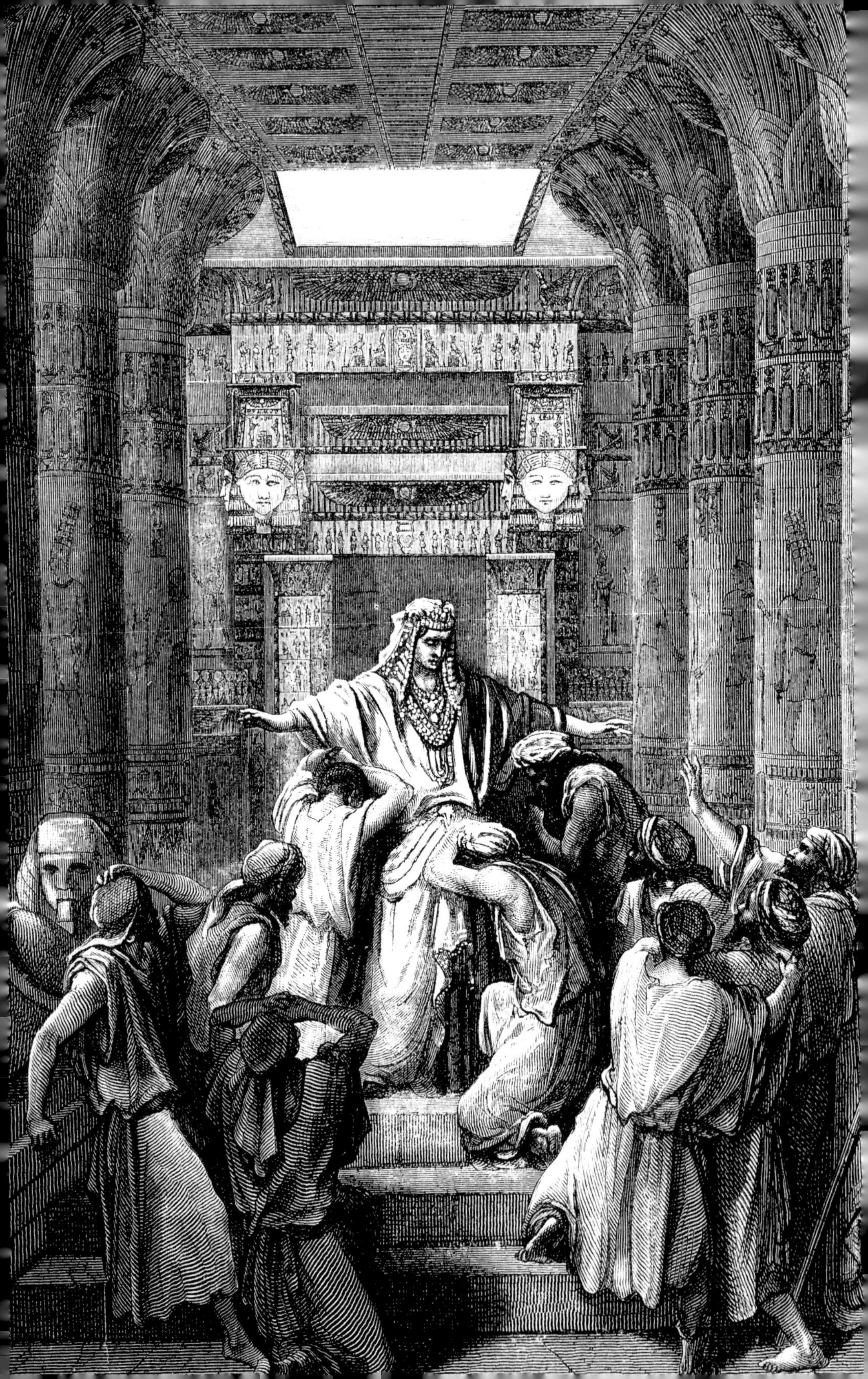

JOSEPH

Chapter 8: Faith for Joseph
Hebrews 11:22

Hebrews 11:22 – By faith Joseph, at the end of his life, made mention of the exodus of the Israelites and gave directions concerning his bones.

Imagine a long road trip where most of the journey is spent driving fast on the highway while the sites quickly pass, but you occasionally slow down to see the sights, and, once in a while, you pull over to take in some special scenery. Genesis is like that.

Genesis 1-2 covered the entirety of Creation, focusing on Adam and Eve. Genesis 1-14 covers roughly 1000 years, including Noah and his family, while also introducing Abraham and Sarah. The covenantal blessing on Joseph's family started with Abraham, and God promised that their family would be blessed by God to be a blessing to the nations. That prophecy begins to be fulfilled with Joseph blessing the nation of Egypt.

Genesis 14-36 covers another roughly 1000 years, looking at Joseph's great-grandfather Abraham, his grandfather Isaac, and his father Jacob, who had 13 children (12 sons and one daughter) with two wives (who were sisters) as well as concubines in what is a dysfunctional family of epic proportions. The backdrop for Joseph's story is family strife marked by parental favoritism and a young man who is a bit spoiled and arrogant but who has a unique anointing and calling on his life. Genesis does not tell us just what happened but what always happens, and this family story has been played out in every generation since. Their blended family with favoritism and jealousy, lying and covert behavior, and sibling rivalry and factious divisions sounds a lot like many families in our own day. There is a lot of pain throughout the testimony of Joseph, but it's also a remarkable story of forgiveness, healing, and reconciliation.

Joseph's Faith

Joseph is a good man, but he's not Jesus. At times, Joseph suffered because of his own arrogance. Often, however, Joseph suffered because of evil and injustice committed against him. He went from being loved and spoiled in his family that worshiped God to a slave in another nation with no rights and not knowing the language or believing in their demon gods. His own brothers sold him into slavery to another nation and lied, telling their father he was dead. Joseph would not see his beloved dad for two decades, and his father would go into deep despair mourning a son he wrongly thought was dead. It's one thing to be disowned by your family and even worse to also be destroyed by them. This is precisely what happened. Joseph was wrongly convicted of sexual assault, even though it was all a lie, and spent time in jail as a convicted criminal. Joseph's obedience to God is "rewarded" by Potiphar, who was a high-ranking leader in the Egyptian government where Joseph was a slave, with rage and punishment—he is seized and placed in the Pharaoh's prison for allegedly raping his wife—something Joseph never did and she lied about.

The godly virgin is now a convicted rapist and registered sex offender. Joseph is sent to prison for refusing to sleep with Potiphar's wife and rejecting her advances. A fellow inmate, whom Joseph served by interpreting dreams, forgot about him and did not return the favor. Joseph was forced to grow up, marry a woman he did not choose, and raise his children in a nation that was not his own—speaking a foreign language and surrounded by the worship of demonic false gods.

Joseph had a lifetime of opportunities to choose bitterness, unforgiveness, and vengeance. He did not seek vengeance on those who did evil to him. He did not use the pain of his life to excuse rebellious and sinful behavior in response to unjust suffering. He did not embrace the lifelong identity of a victim seeking pity and attention. Instead, Joseph chose forgiveness over and over throughout his life, and God honored that every time.

By the end of his life, Joseph has literally traveled from a pit to a prison to a palace. His life goes from being a broke and powerless slave to one of the most powerful and wealthiest men in the world. The only reason Joseph could lead and love at such a high level is because of the depth of forgiveness he had extended throughout his life. Had Joseph not invited the Holy Spirit to unburden and emotionally heal him, he would have remained a bitter and broken believer and certainly would not have been ready for the task of leading a nation and saving his family from famine.

Genesis 37-50 covers roughly 100 years of Joseph's life. The life of Joseph is epic. In it we see a dysfunctional family, a passive father, betrayal, slavery, sexual temptation, an undeserved prison sentence, prophetic dreams, political intrigue, forgiveness, and a family reunion after 20 years of painful separation.

As we come to Genesis 48, Joseph's father, Jacob, is nearing the end of his life. Jacob is not a guy who has done it all the right way. In fact, he's not even a guy who has done it *mostly the right way*. He raised a dumpster fire of a family, with the exception of Joseph, and it was by the grace and providence of God alone that finally reunited Jacob with all of his sons in one big happy family. The old man mustered up the strength to sit up in bed to remind his son and grandson of how El Shaddai ("God almighty") appeared to him in Luz (the older name for Bethel) and blessed him with the promises of the covenant first spoken to his grandfather Abraham. During this visit, Jacob elevated Joseph's two sons as tribes of Israel along with Joseph and his brothers. In an incredibly rich chapter dripping with emotion, as the sons are reunited around the bedside of their dying dad, Joseph gets to say goodbye, be blessed by his dad, and have his sons blessed by their grandpa as Jacob tells stories at the age of 147 about how much he loves and misses his wife, Rachel. The rich kindness of God is on full display.

In the closing scene of Joseph's testimony, his brothers are fearful that he will punish them in bitterness. After a famine hit their homeland, Joseph's family moved to Egypt to avoid starving to death. At first, the brothers did not recognize Joseph because he was a grown man and Egyptian royalty. He, however, also knew their language, overhearing their conversation in Hebrew, and had to excuse himself to weep after not seeing his brothers for decades. Joseph had forgiven his brothers, but he had to test them so he could trust them. The brothers demonstrated repentance, regretted the evil they had done to him, and reconciled with him. However, after their father died, the brothers worried that Joseph was in fact unforgiving and would then enact his justice. In one of the most moving scenes in the Bible, it says in Genesis 50:19-21,

> But Joseph said to them, "Do not fear, for am I in the place of God? As for you, you meant evil against me, but God meant it for good, to bring it about that many people should be kept alive, as they are today. So do not fear; I will provide for you and your little ones." Thus he comforted them and spoke kindly to them.

You know you have forgiven someone when you can bless them. This is precisely how God treats us; although we have sinned against Him, our Lord not only forgives us but also blesses us. Joseph was sold by his brothers into slavery at the age of 17. Joseph lived to be 110 years of age, a blessed man who got to bounce his great-grandsons on his knee. Though imperfect, Joseph is one of the greatest men with the highest character in human history.

Joseph's Failure

Jacob did not even seek to conceal his favoritism for Joseph, lavishly adorning the second-to-youngest son with an expensive coat of many colors, like some ancient Hebrew hip-hop homie. Jacob also placed Joseph in authority over his older brothers by sending him out into the fields to oversee their work and report back to their father. Because Jacob plays favorites with his sons, Joseph feels free to "tattle" on his brothers when they mess up.

Imagine being a kid in that family where your youngest brother not only reports on everything you do to get you in trouble but then Dad rewards him for it with an expensive gift that distinguishes him like a proud peacock as the favored son. Curiously, Genesis tells us that Joseph's brothers didn't hate their father for his favoritism but hated Joseph for being the favorite. When we play favorites as parents, we are pitting our kids against each other and creating factions in our own homes. However, even though a young man, Joseph also bears some responsibility, along with his father, because he enjoyed being the favorite and acted a bit like a spoiled brat with his brothers.

God had also given the young Joseph dreams in which his whole family was bowing down in homage to him. Rather than keeping that information to himself, the young and perhaps impetuous Joseph told his brothers, which only made matters worse. Throughout Genesis 37, we continually read that his brothers hated him, were jealous of him, and could not speak a kind word to him because they despised him so intensely. While not excusing the sin of his brothers, this sense of spoiled entitlement is a flaw in the character of young Joseph that God had to work out of his soul to make him a great leader.

Our Faithful God

The Egyptian empire, which serves as the scene for the life of Joseph, was the most powerful on earth for an amazing 1300 years, twice as long as the famed Greek and Roman empires. Egypt was ruled by a succession of mighty Pharaohs who were worshiped as mediator gods who connected life on the earth to life in the spirit realm and alone walked between the two worlds—a counterfeit of Christ. As deities, the pharaohs had burial pyramids built to ensure their safe passage from this world to the next as a sort of ladder transporting their soul into the next world. Simply, there was no nation on earth more powerful than Egypt, and there was no man in Egypt more powerful than the Pharaoh, whose will was supreme.

What the Egyptians didn't know was that Joseph's God was in fact supreme because He alone could give dreams, He alone could interpret those dreams, and the future that He promised could not be thwarted by anyone, including the mighty

Pharaoh. Therefore, Joseph's God was supreme to even the Pharaoh and had sent Joseph to Egypt as a sort of missionary to bless that nation according to His covenant promise to bless the nations of the earth.

For believers, a main point of the Joseph story is that God continuously works through providence and sometimes miracles. When you think of God's work in your life, remember that He has two proverbial hands: a visible hand of miracle, working in your life with obvious supernatural displays of power, and an invisible hand of providence, working in your life with subtle, behind-the-scenes planning and care.

God works in Joseph's life most often through His unseen hand of providence. This explains why, despite all the trials, Joseph is ruling in Egypt to save that nation, along with his own extended family of 66 people, from starvation, thereby preserving the descendants of Abraham. Over 400 years later, God would allow them to leave Egypt as a nation of millions, ready to occupy the Promised Land and preserved to bring forth Jesus Christ into the world through that family line.

Joseph succeeds because, even though he doesn't have an absence of trouble, he has the presence of God. In Genesis 39, for example, the presence of God in Joseph's life is mentioned five times. Joseph succeeds because, as he walks with God and conducts himself in obedience to authority, God works through him and providentially orders the things around him to work in his favor and the future favor of God's people. Although everyone had abused and abandoned Joseph, we read that God remained with him, blessed him, and caused him to prosper according to His covenant promises.

Throughout the testimony of Joseph, the themes of God's providence and presence are repeatedly highlighted. God's sovereign providence over his life and the Holy Spirit's work in and through him are the secrets to his success.

- Genesis 39:2—The Lord was with Joseph, and he became a successful man...
- Genesis 39:3—His master saw that the Lord was with him and that the Lord caused all that he did to succeed in his

hands.
- Genesis 39:5— … the Lord blessed the Egyptian's house for Joseph's sake; the blessing of the Lord was on all that he had…
- Genesis 39:23—The keeper of the prison paid no attention to anything that was in Joseph's charge, because the Lord was with him. And whatever he did, the Lord made it succeed.
- Genesis 41:38—Pharaoh said to his servants, "Can we find a man like this, in whom is the Spirit of God?"

The testimony of Joseph is that the most important thing any believer has is the anointing and powerful favor of God's providence over and presence in our lives. His Holy Spirit anointing is more valuable than any wealth or wisdom, power or prestige. Joseph lost everything but one thing. He lost his nation, father, brothers, family, freedom, reputation, and decades of his life. He did not, however, lose his anointing. God's anointing was so great on Joseph because his forgiveness was so deep.

Like Joseph, Jesus loved those who hated Him and suffered unjustly at the hands of those who were jealous. But, just as in the days of Joseph, God transformed what sinners intended for evil into good, fulfilling His original intention for creation and leading to the salvation of many lives through Jesus.[a]

At the end of his life, Jesus, like Joseph before Him, spoke words of kindness, blessing, and forgiveness from His cross to His enemies, thereby making them friends and brothers. Jesus, like Joseph before Him, was buried in a tomb. Unlike Joseph, who remains buried today, the Lord Jesus Christ rose from death in triumphant victory over sin. In so doing, Jesus proved that He was the covenant God of Abraham, Isaac, and Jacob, as well as his son Joseph.

By living in the anointing of the Spirit, there are many ways that Joseph's testimony is a bit like Jesus':

[a] Genesis 50:20

1. Joseph and Jesus were both sons loved by their earthly and heavenly fathers.
2. Joseph and Jesus were both chosen to be the firstborn son.
3. Joseph and Jesus were both sons chosen by the Heavenly Father to save and rule.
4. Joseph and Jesus were both taken to Egypt as young men.
5. Joseph and Jesus were both shepherds (a shepherd and the Good Shepherd).
6. Joseph and Jesus had family that did not believe their destiny.
7. Joseph and Jesus were hated by their jealous brothers.
8. Joseph and Jesus were sold for pieces of silver like the price of a slave (20 and 30 pieces of silver, respectively).
9. Joseph and Jesus were both stripped of their clothing.
10. Joseph and Jesus both had a robe dipped in blood (Genesis 37:31, Revelation 19:13).
11. Joseph and Jesus were both thrown in a hole.
12. Joseph and Jesus were both separated from their father (Joseph earthly, Jesus heavenly).
13. Joseph and Jesus forgave those who sinned against them.
14. Joseph and Jesus both ruled over kingdoms from the right hand of the king.
15. Joseph and Jesus both brought a multitude of life and grace by getting out of their hole they were left for dead in.
16. Joseph is worshiping Jesus right now in the Kingdom.

Thus far in Hebrews 11, we have learned from the people listed in Genesis, the first book of the Bible. Next, we will turn the page and learn about Moses, who was born in Egypt some 400 years after Joseph, as the family of Jacob has grown to become an enslaved nation.

Dig Deeper.
1. To learn more about Joseph, read Genesis 37-50.

Walk it out. Talk it out.
1. What most surprises you about the faith and failures of Joseph?
2. Who do you personally know that reminds you a bit of Joseph—someone who has suffered great injustice but remains godly and forgiving?
3. Are there any relationships you have with extended family members that remind you of the story of Joseph with his brothers?
4. Is there anyone that you need to forgive, as Joseph did?
5. How can group members be praying for one another this week?

HEBREWS 11

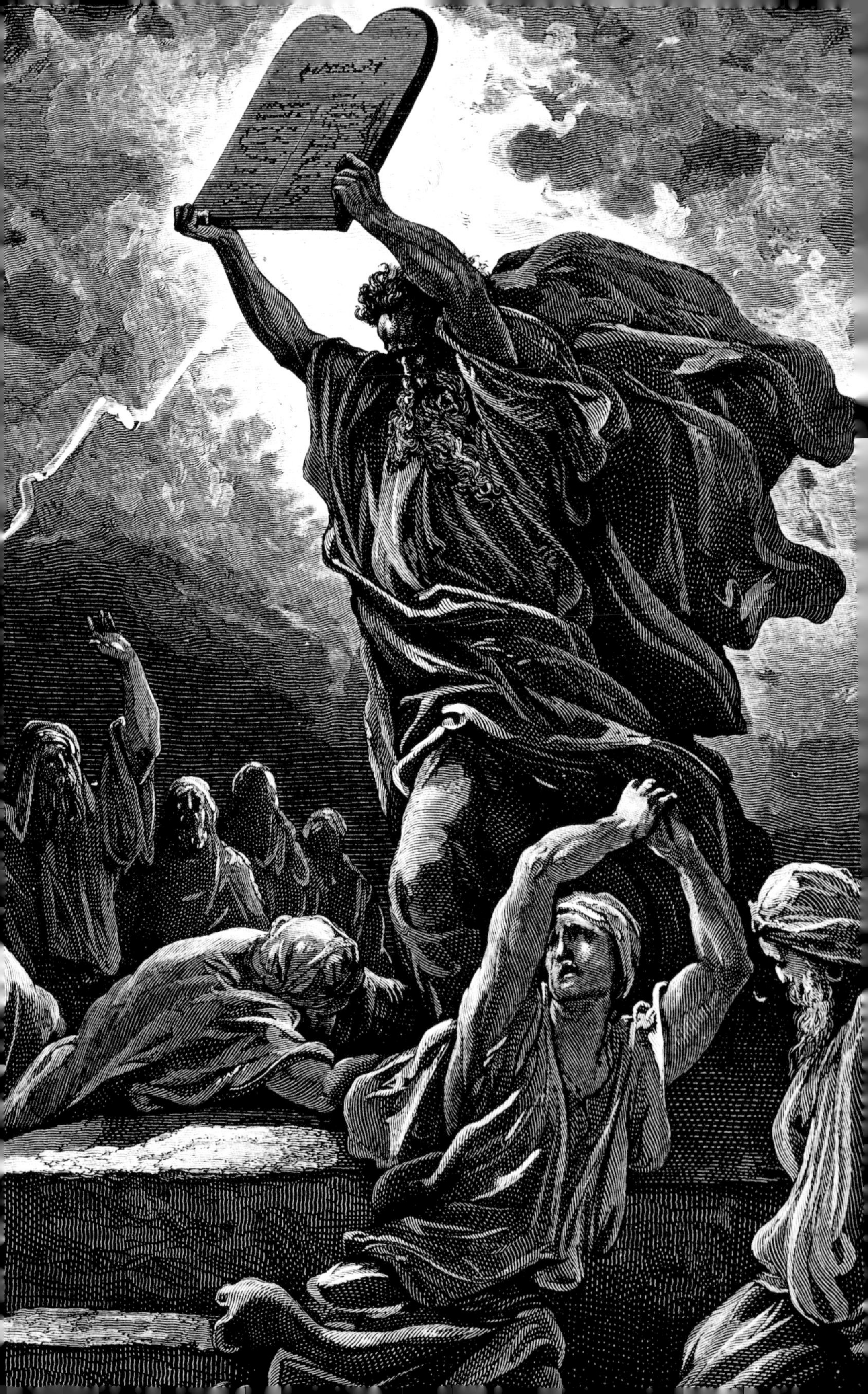

MOSES

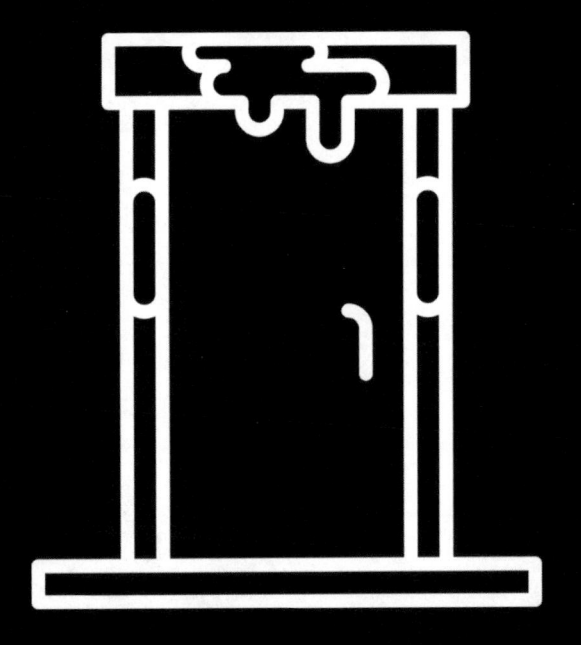

Chapter 9: Faith for Moses
Hebrews 11:23-29

Hebrews 11:23-29 – By faith Moses, when he was born, was hidden for three months by his parents, because they saw that the child was beautiful, and they were not afraid of the king's edict. By faith Moses, when he was grown up, refused to be called the son of Pharaoh's daughter, choosing rather to be mistreated with the people of God than to enjoy the fleeting pleasures of sin. He considered the reproach of Christ greater wealth than the treasures of Egypt, for he was looking to the reward. By faith he left Egypt, not being afraid of the anger of the king, for he endured as seeing him who is invisible. By faith he kept the Passover and sprinkled the blood, so that the Destroyer of the firstborn might not touch them. By faith the people crossed the Red Sea as on dry land, but the Egyptians, when they attempted to do the same, were drowned.

In the United States, we honor some of our most prominent presidents at a national monument called Mount Rushmore. The massive sculpture on the side of a mountain has the carved faces of four men—George Washington, Abraham Lincoln, Thomas Jefferson, and Theodore Roosevelt. If there were the same kind of monument for heroes in the Old Testament, Moses would have to be included.

Considered by many to be the most prominent person in the Old Testament, Moses was chosen by God to lead a few million Hebrew people out of bondage and slavery in Egypt, paving the way for the founding of the nation of Israel. In the wilderness, he led God's people for 40 years, receiving the 10 Commandments directly from God, and bringing them to the edge of the Promised Land divinely pledged to Abraham's descendants in the Abrahamic Covenant. Moses lived roughly 1400 years before Christ, which was roughly 3500 years ago.

Moses' story begins in the book of Exodus and continues in Leviticus, Numbers, and Deuteronomy. The Exodus narrative opens amid the Hebrew peoples' slavery under a tyrannical Pharaoh of Egypt (1:1-15:21). Unlike the days of Joseph, who lived 400 years prior, this Pharaoh did not remember or respect their God.

Moses' Faith

Moses serves as a great prophet of God[a] whom the Holy Spirit worked through to pen the first five books of the Bible (also called the Pentateuch or "book in five parts"). Moses' life was spared as a baby by God's providence when his mother, Jochebed, hid him in a basket on the banks of the Nile River to spare him from a governmental decree to kill the Hebrew baby boys. In God's sovereignty, it was King Pharaoh's daughter who found Moses and raised him as her son.[b] Moses was then given an extraordinary education[c] and the privileges that come with being raised in a royal family. Around the age of 40, after killing a man, Moses fled from Egypt to Midian, near Sinai, where he lived a private life with his wife as a shepherd.[d] At the age of 80, Moses returned to Egypt, by faith, in obedience to God's call. God intended to use him in the judgment of the nation of Egypt for enslaving and mistreating His people, leading them to deliverance and freedom to worship and return to their homeland.

Hebrews 11:23–29 presents Moses as the central figure of Israel's deliverance—a prophet, lawgiver, and redeemer. Moses is sustained by faith amid fear, compromise, exile, and eventual obedience. Like Abraham, Moses operates in response to divine promise, not visible outcome. Each moment—rejection, endurance, courage, obedience—reveals his faith as forward-facing fidelity in the face of peril.

The Egyptians were such a polytheistic and varied people with so many competing demonic gods and pagan priests that any attempt to formulate a codified religious system was virtually impossible. There was no concept of a supreme singular God but rather a multitude of local deities. Each town had its own deity, and every object and phenomenon of nature, like a crocodile or fish, was thought to be infused with a spirit that could choose its physical form. The Egyptians held several

[a] Deuteronomy 34:10 [b] Exodus 1-2 [c] Acts 7:22 [d] Exodus 2-3

animals sacred, including the bull, cow, cat, baboon, jackal, and crocodile. Some deities were composites of humans and animals, such as Thoth, who had the head of an ibis; Horus, who had the head of a hawk; or the a, carved out of one rock with the body of a lion and the head of a man.

There was also no division between sacred and secular within Egyptian society, leading to the creation of beautiful art and breathtaking architecture intended to bring people closer to the gods. Among the handful of gods who had a wider impact beyond their local recognition were Ra and Osiris. Ra, the sun god, was the most important and recognized as the giver of life.

Conversely, the Hebrews had one God who was not in need of service but instead served people. Their God was not fed by human food but instead fed His people with manna from Heaven. Their God also lived in a tabernacle aimed not at housing Himself for leisure but instead at inviting His people for rest and forgiveness of sin. The service to this God was also conducted by a priest, but not a priest who worked for the god but rather a priest who labored for the people before God. Hebrews defines Moses' faith not just by inactive belief but also by active behavior. Each verse in Hebrews 11 highlights a specific moment where Moses or those around him choose God's promise over immediate safety, prestige, or security.

By faith, Moses' parents hid him.[a] Though the verse centers on Moses, it is his unnamed parents—Amram and Jochebed[b]—whose faith is commended. They recognized that the child was "beautiful," and their refusal to obey Pharaoh's decree stems from a holy defiance. The phrase "they were not afraid of the king's edict" echoes Hebrews' recurring motif of reverent fear versus slavish terror.[c] Faith, in this context, is fearless obedience to God's hidden work.

By faith, Moses, when he was grown up, refused to be called a son of Pharaoh's daughter.[d] The phrase "son of Pharaoh's daughter" signals more than adoption; it denotes full integration into the Egyptian elite. Moses' rejection is thus a renunciation of identity, privilege, and political power. Faith

---

[a] Heb 11:23 [b] Exod 6:20 [c] cf. Heb 10:27; 12:28 [d] Heb 11:24

here is not an abstract belief in God's existence but a concrete act of disassociation for the sake of God's people. By standing with God, Moses was standing against the entire royal family and nation that raised him.

By faith, Moses chose to share ill-treatment with the people of God.[a] This act of humility volunteers Moses to suffer great loss, endure great pain, and risk his own life and family. He does not merely witness Israel's plight—he enters it. Instead of "the fleeting pleasures of sin," he embraces what is costly, painful, and impossible unless God shows up in power. The sin referred to is not generic immorality but the seduction of Egyptian power and pleasure. Faith, then, is enduring loss in light of future gain.

By faith, "[h]e considered the reproach of Christ greater wealth than the treasures of Egypt."[b] This verse reaches the summit of faith. Moses' faith is reinterpreted in light of his confidence in the coming of Christ over 1400 years before He was born of Mary! Amazingly, by faith, Moses believed in the coming of Christ to suffer and die for sinners and was willing to suffer and die for Christ—and to some degree, *like* Christ! Moses received supernatural revelation about Christ and believed it by faith.

Moses has the long view of things: "…he was looking to the reward." Moses looked forward to the first coming of Christ and into the future Second Coming of Christ. By faith, Moses was living for and looking to the rule and reign of Jesus Christ over all—roughly 3500 plus years into the future! The word ("recompense") ties back to Hebrews 10:35 and 11:6, where reward is promised to those who seek God. Faith, again, is forward-facing: it sees what is promised, though unseen.
By faith, Moses left Egypt. Hebrews 11:27 says he was "not… afraid of the anger of the king…" In Exodus 2:14-15, it was said of Moses:

> He answered, "Who made you a prince and a judge over us? Do you mean to kill me as you killed the Egyptian?"

---

[a] Heb 11:25 [b] Heb 11:26

Then Moses was afraid, and thought, "Surely the thing is known." When Pharaoh heard of it, he sought to kill Moses. But Moses fled from Pharaoh and stayed in the land of Midian.

The commentary in Hebrews 11 on Exodus 2 shows us that, although Moses began with fear, he moved to faith. This is a great lesson for every believer—there will be times when we are moved by fear, but we need not stay in fear; we can always remove and replace fear with faith.

By faith, Moses "kept the Passover and sprinkled the blood..."[a] In Exodus 12, Moses leads Israel in observing the first Passover, marking their doorposts with blood to escape the destroyer. This anticipates Hebrews' broader theology of sacrificial blood.[b] Here, Moses' faith is revealed in acts of worship and trust is enacted in worshipful obedience.

Faith includes rituals like the ancient Passover that was replaced with Communion by Jesus at the Last Supper, where He applied Passover to being fulfilled in His sacrifice on the cross[c]—not as empty symbols but as visible trust in invisible deliverance. By faith, the people passed through the Red Sea following the faith of Moses, their leader.[d] This verse transitions from Moses to the collective. Israel's passage through the sea[e] becomes a communal act of faith. The sea became "dry land," yet only those who trusted God's word crossed safely. The Egyptian army attempting to do the same was swallowed up. The contrast between faithful obedience and faithless presumption is clear. Faith, again, is not mystical—it is movement. Israel walks forward into impossibility, trusting the God who parts the waters.

Moses serves as the primary example of faith in Exodus, but not the only example of faith. Others have faith in God and they join Moses in standing against evil for the good of others and the glory of God. The lesson here is simple but significant: faith is contagious, and if one person stands in faith, especially a leader, others will do the same. At the end of Exodus 1, the

---

[a] Heb 11:28 [b] cf. Heb 9:12-14 [c] Matthew 26:17-29 [d] Heb 11:29 [e] Exodus 14

Hebrew midwives Shiphrah and Puah appear as the first heroes in the book. We are told that they, unlike Pharaoh, feared God and sought to serve God by not killing the Hebrew children.

Moses' mother makes her entrance at the beginning of chapter 2. She demonstrates her love for her son and faith in God as she places him in a reed basket, floating him down the Nile in the face of otherwise certain death at the hands of Pharaoh.

Moses' brother, Aaron, enters the story in the middle of chapter 4 and becomes a primary character both in Exodus and throughout the Bible as a man of faith and the line through which the priesthood is drawn. Moses' sister, Miriam, who was first mentioned as watching Moses' reed basket float down the Nile in chapter 2, appears again at the end of chapter 15 to lead the nation in worship of God as a great woman of faith. Moses' young protégé, Joshua, appears in the middle of chapter 17 and grows to become a very prominent Old Testament hero. He is also mentioned in Hebrews 11:30 as a man of great faith in connection with the falling of the Jericho walls.

Moses' Failure

Moses' life unfolds in the shadow of profound political, personal, and spiritual tensions. While Moses is a man of incredible faith, he is also a sinner—flawed like the rest of us—and, on some occasions, he demonstrates failure instead of faith. His failure is not one of godlessness but of impulse, isolation, and delay. This should be encouraging—we can all relate to Moses if we are honest.

When Moses sees an Egyptian beating a Hebrew, he kills the man.[a] The act is rash and uncoordinated—driven more by zeal than divine commission. The Hebrews reject him, asking, "Who made you a prince and a judge over us?"[b] His misplaced timing forces him into exile in Midian, where he remains for 40 years.[c] In fleeing Pharaoh's wrath[d], Moses begins a pattern of withdrawal that continues even into his divine calling—marked

---

[a] Exodus 2:11-12 [b] Exodus 2:14 [c] Acts 7:30 [d] Exodus 2:15

by resistance, insecurity, and protest.[a]

Even at the height of his leadership, Moses' faith coexists with complaint. After initial failure before Pharaoh and rejection by the people[b], he questions God's purpose. When finally leading Israel into freedom, his own impulsiveness resurfaces. In Numbers 20:10-13, striking the rock in frustration rather than speaking as instructed disqualifies him from entering the Promised Land. Since the nation was watching, God made an example of Moses with consequences for his pride and sin in that instance. The punishment was severe, but as a leader, Moses was held to a higher standard because he was setting an example for all the people. These events reveal the fragility and complexity of Moses' faith. He is not a flawless liberator but a man formed through rejection, delay, and divine patience. He's an amazing man but still a man.

<u>Our Faithful God</u>

Regarding the days of Moses' faith, God says in Micah 6:4, "I brought you up from the land of Egypt and redeemed you from the house of slavery, and I sent before you Moses, Aaron, and Miriam." Sovereignly at work in the days of Moses was his faithful God. It was God who worked through Moses as the hero of the Exodus.

One of the primary purposes of the Exodus deliverance was to reveal God in glory to both His people and their enemies. 1 Samuel 2:27 says, "And there came a man of God to Eli and said to him, 'Thus says the Lord, "Did I indeed reveal myself to the house of your father when they were in Egypt subject to the house of Pharaoh?"'" In the events surrounding the life of Moses in the days of the Exodus, God was revealed. The nation who worshiped demonic counterfeit gods learned the painful lesson that the One True Real God could crush their counterfeits and nation with ease.

The hero of Moses' life is God. Moses is a secondary figure

---

[a] Exod. 3:11; 4:1, 10, 13 [b] Exodus 5:19–23

whom God uses to further His purposes and extend His glory, despite Moses' initial unwillingness to obey the call of God on his life. In Egyptian theology, Moses would have been seen as a god to Pharaoh. Exodus 7:1 says, "And the Lord said to Moses, 'See, I have made you like God to Pharaoh, and your brother Aaron shall be your prophet.'" Just as the Egyptians considered their Pharaoh a god, Moses would have been seen as a servant of his God and their conflict as a war between the foreign God of the Hebrews and the gods of Egypt on their own home turf. God, not Moses, was unseating Pharaoh as king and is the true hero of the story.

Throughout the story of Moses' life, God continually reveals Himself as separate and unlike any pagan notion of deity. Demanding allegiance and worship alone, He demonstrates sovereignty over all creation and history.

The first mention of the One True God in the Exodus narrative is of Him being feared (1:17). From there we discover that God is kind (1:20), God hears the cries of the oppressed and cares about their plight (2:23-25), God is a person with a name who speaks to His servant (3:4-6), God promises His presence with His people (3:12), God desires to be worshiped (3:12), God names Himself (3:14), God demands sacrifices be made to Him (3:18), God has unequaled miraculous power (4:8), God makes people as they are (4:11), God will help and teach His servants (4:12), God does kill (4:23), God is not known or feared by all (5:2), God remembers His promises (6:5), God frees His people from bondage (6:6), God takes people to Himself (6:7), God speaks through men (7:2), God can harden hearts (7:3), God is like no one else (8:10), God answers the prayers of His servants (8:13; 8:31), God expects to be worshiped as He commands (8:27), God never fails to keep His word (9:5-6), God alone does not sin (9:27), God deals harshly with the unrepentant (10:2), God detests all false gods (12:12), God goes before His people (13:21), God wants glory for Himself (14:4), God fights for His people (14:14; 14:25), God gains glory even through unholy people (14:17), God commands even nature (14:21), God has great power (14:31), God is highly exalted (15:1), God is strength, song, and salvation (15:2), God is a warrior (15:3), God is majestic in power (15:6), God has burning anger (15:7), God is like no one else (15:11), God is majestic in holiness (15:11), God is awesome in glory (15:11), God works wonders (15:11), God has unfailing love (15:13), God will reign forever and ever as king (15:18), God provides for the needs of His people (16:4), God is our Banner (17:15), God helps many generations (18:4), God is greater than all other gods (18:11), God has a will, decrees, and laws (18:15-16), God is to be feared (18:21), God owns the whole earth (19:5), God desires a kingdom of priests and a holy nation (19:6), God deeply cares about the conduct of His people (20:1-17), God tests His people so they will fear Him and not sin (20:20), God will not accept false gods alongside of Him (20:23), God cares about injustice and demands restitution (21:12-23:19), God hates blasphemy of His name (22:28), God fills people with His Spirit to empower them to create beauty (31:1-11), God makes covenants with His people (34:10), God names himself Jealous (34:14), and God is sovereign (34:23). The final mention of God in the Exodus narrative is of His glory being revealed amongst His people (40:34-35).

    Pharaoh mockingly asked, "Who is the Lord, that I should obey him and let Israel go? I do not know the Lord…"[a] In a moment of ignorance and arrogance, Pharaoh asked the fateful question, "Who is the Lord?" God took this challenge seriously and used the entire Exodus story as His answer. At every turn in the plot, God is revealed. The primary theme of Exodus does not revolve around Moses or the Exodus event, but rather the revelation of God that He might be known, feared, and worshiped by Egypt and Israel alike. All other events in the story, such as the birth of Moses and deliverance through the sea, are secondary events through which God reveals Himself. God Himself declared this by saying, "…the Egyptians shall know that I am the Lord, when I have gotten glory over Pharaoh, his chariots, and his horsemen."[b]

    The plot of Exodus that serves as the backdrop of Moses' life and ministry is nothing less than a cosmic showdown

---

[a] Exod 5:2 [b] Exod 14:18

between God and Satan. God is the primary character that makes His entrance personally in Exodus 3:14-15 by appearing to Moses and revealing His name as YHWH:

> God said to Moses, "I am who I am." And he said, "Say this to the people of Israel: 'I am has sent me to you.'" God also said to Moses, "Say this to the people of Israel: 'The Lord, the God of your fathers, the God of Abraham, the God of Isaac, and the God of Jacob, has sent me to you.' This is my name forever, and thus I am to be remembered throughout all generations."

In Hebrew understanding, the name embodies the entire essence and identity of a person. So, in having a name, God revealed Himself as a person and gave sacred access to an understanding and experience of His very person. Jesus later takes this same name in John 8:58 to designate Himself as that person revealed as YHWH in the burning bush: "Jesus said to them, 'Truly, truly, I say to you, before Abraham was, I am.'" Understanding Jesus claimed to be the God who spoke to Moses years prior, those who heard him found him guilty of blasphemy, and "they picked up stones to throw at him, but Jesus hid himself and went out of the temple." Jesus said He was the God of Moses, and this was not wrongful blasphemy but rather truthful testimony.

Perhaps the most obvious way that God reveals Himself throughout the life of Moses is in the numerous miracles that He accomplishes. The life of Moses is one of the most supernatural seasons in all of Scripture. Here is a list of God's miracles that surrounded Moses:

1. God speaks to Moses in the burning Bush (Exodus 3)
2. Rod becomes a snake (Exodus 4:3-4, 7:8-12)
3. Moses' hand becomes leprous (Exodus 4:6-7)
4. First plague: water turned into blood (Exodus 4:9, 7:14-25)
5. Second plague: frogs (Exodus 8:1-15)
6. Third plague: lice (Exodus 8:16-19)

7. Fourth plague: flies (Exodus 8:20-32)
8. Fifth plague: pestilence destroys livestock (Exodus 9:1-7)
9. Sixth plague: boils (Exodus 9:8-12)
10. Seventh plague: hail (Exodus 9:13-35)
11. Eighth plague: locusts (Exodus 10:1-20)
12. Ninth plague: darkness (Exodus 10:21-29)
13. Tenth plague: firstborn sons die (Exodus 11:1-12:36)
14. Parting the Red Sea (Exodus 14:1-31)
15. Bitter water made sweet (Exodus 15:22-25)
16. Manna from Heaven (Numbers 11:1-9)
17. Quail to eat (Exodus 16:8-13)
18. Water from a rock (Exodus 17:1-7)
19. Defeating the Amalekites (Exodus 17:8-13)
20. Quenches the fire of death (Numbers 11:2)
21. Miriam is healed (Numbers 12:13-15)
22. Earth swallows Korah and the rebels (Numbers 16:28-33)
23. Moses ends the plague (Numbers 16:44-50)
24. Water from a rock (Numbers 20:7-13)
25. Saved from snakes (Numbers 21:5-9)

These miracles reveal God in glory. God also receives glory through the transformation of Moses, the deliverance of His people, and the anticipation of Christ. In Moses' parents, we see God glorified through humble courage. Their defiance of Pharaoh becomes the first sign of divine reversal: fear of God overrules fear of man. In Moses' rejection of Egypt, God is glorified through allegiance. Moses' solidarity with God's people magnifies the God who is not ashamed to be called their God.[a] His willingness to suffer loss anticipates the messianic pattern: loss for glory, death for life. Moses, in refusing Pharaoh, becomes an icon of the Christ who "though he was rich…became poor."[b] God's glory is further revealed in Moses' vision of the invisible. By lifting his eyes to the unseen, he shows that God is worth more than an empire. This glorifies the

---

[a] Heb 11:16 [b] 2 Cor 8:9

God who is eternal, invisible, and faithful. At Passover, God's glory shines in substitution. Blood on doorposts becomes a sign of judgment diverted—a foretaste of the Lamb whose blood will shield from death.[a] Moses leads Israel not merely in ritual but in reverent obedience that honors God's provision.

Finally, in the Red Sea crossing, God's power is made manifest. Salvation is not merely an escape—it is a demonstration of sovereign grace. In the Exodus, as well as the Second Coming of Christ as the greater Moses, two things occur. One, God's people are delivered, blessed, and provided for. Two, their enemies are destroyed and crushed forever. The contrast with Egypt—destroyed by the same waters that delivered Israel—underscores that faith is not generic trust but trust in the living, acting God. In all of this, faith is how God's people align with God's action. The hero is not Moses. The hero is God—the one who sees, saves, speaks, and sends. When Jesus was on the earth roughly 1400 years after Moses, Moses made an astonishing brief return visit from Heaven. Matthew 17:1-5 says,

> And after six days Jesus took with him Peter and James, and John his brother, and led them up a high mountain by themselves. And he was transfigured before them, and his face shone like the sun, and his clothes became white as light. And behold, there appeared to them Moses and Elijah, talking with him. And Peter said to Jesus, "Lord, it is good that we are here. If you wish, I will make three tents here, one for you and one for Moses and one for Elijah." He was still speaking when, behold, a bright cloud overshadowed them, and a voice from the cloud said, "This is my beloved Son, with whom I am well pleased; listen to him."

In this scene, Moses is honored by Christ. Even though Moses did not get to enter the Promised Land, he did enter the Kingdom of God with Jesus Christ. Moses' faith was in

---

[a] cf. John 1:29

Jesus Christ, who was faithful to get him out of Egypt and into Heaven and brought him back to earth with Him for a visit to honor His faithful servant.

Dig Deeper.

1. To learn more about Moses, read the following chapters in Exodus: 1-4 (slavery and Moses' call), 12-17 (the Exodus and God's provision), 19-24 (the Ten Commandments and covenant laws), and 32-34 and 40 (being in God's presence).

Walk it out. Talk it out.

1. What most surprised you about Moses' faith and failure? Why?
2. What are the personal lessons you can learn from the life of Moses?
3. If you could have been present for one scene of Moses' life, which one would it be?
4. How can group members be praying for each other this week?

HEBREWS 11

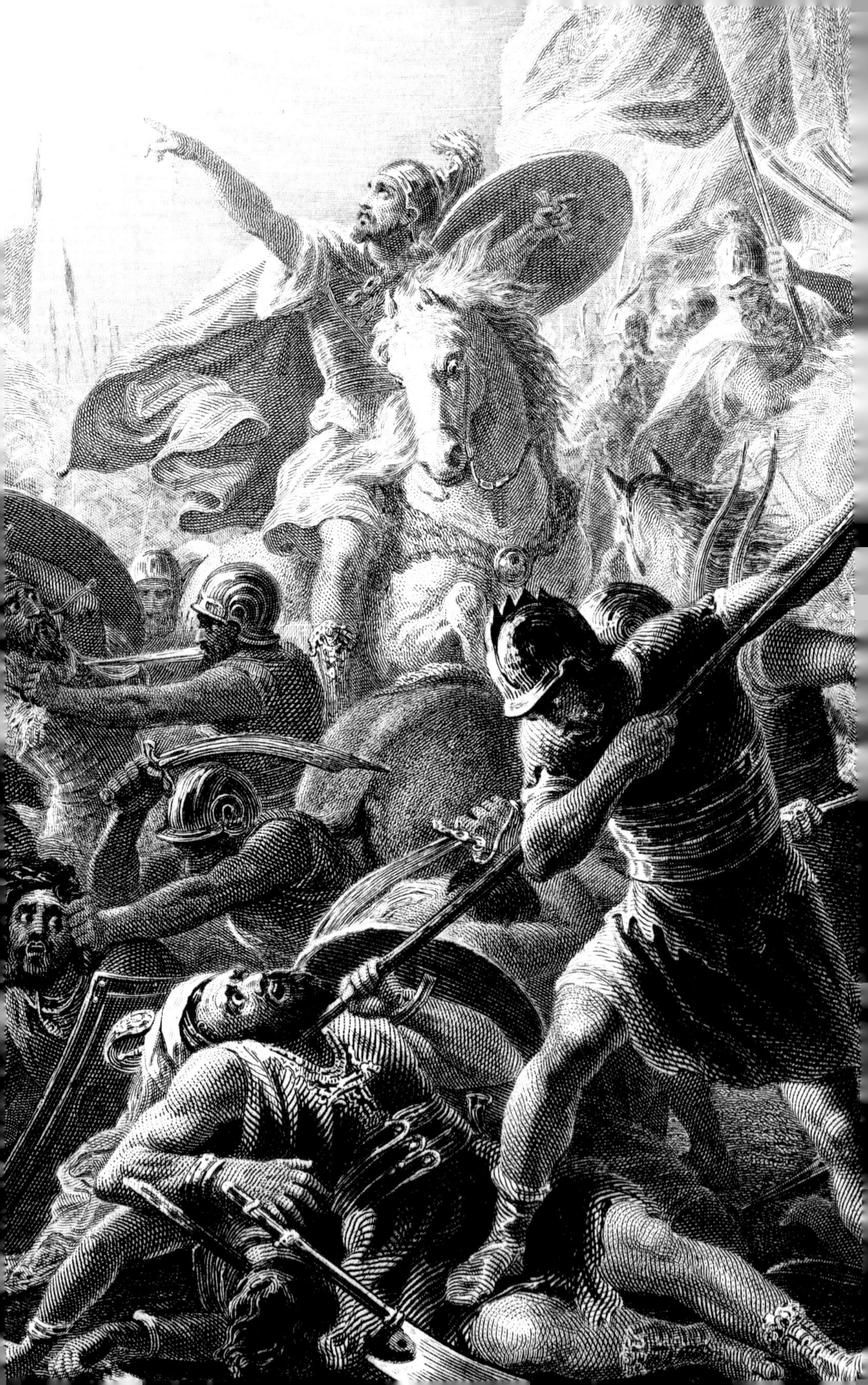

JOSHUA

Chapter 10: Faith for Joshua
Hebrews 11:30

Hebrews 11:30 – By faith the walls of Jericho fell down after they had been encircled for seven days.

When you turn a page in the Bible, sometimes you are moving decades or even centuries into the future. God works over time, patiently bringing His promises to pass. This is precisely what happens between the end of Genesis and the beginning of the next book of the Bible, Exodus, and yet again as the story of God's faithfulness moves from Exodus to the book of Joshua.

In this section of Hebrews, the author has moved us from the promise to Abraham and Sarah of a covenant that included the Promised Land to the entrance and occupation of that land 600 or more years later. After spending more than 400 years in Egypt from the days of Joseph to the deliverance from bondage by God through Moses, the generation that was freed from slavery spent 40 years wandering in the wilderness during what should have been an 11-day journey.[a]

Why did an 11-day walk take 40 years? Because of their grievous sin described in Numbers 13-14, referred to as the "rebellion," where the people despised God, wanted to return to slavery in Egypt, and were routed in battle because God did not go with them into war. Their rebellion, if tolerated by God, would have negated the entire Abrahamic Covenant. They would not have occupied the Promised Land or brought forth the nation of Israel, the priesthood, prophets, Temple, or sacrificial system, all paving the way for the coming of Jesus Christ as the blessing promised to the nations of the earth coming from the nation of Israel.

In addition, the people kept grumbling to God day after day, complaining about Him rather than trusting Him in faith. A Bible dictionary says,

[a] Deuteronomy 1:2

Grumbling is a word that well describes the behaviour pattern of the Exodus generation. Three stories in Exodus 15:22–17:7 set the tone for much of Israel's subsequent behaviour. The Israelites leave Egypt under the most miraculous of circumstances; then, within one month of their departure, they forget the lessons they learned from the Exodus experience.[31]

Despite the people's complaints, God often responded with miraculous provision, such as sweetening the water at Marah when the people complained about their water quality or providing manna and quail in the desert when they complained about their diet. God was gracious to those who were ungrateful to Him, but as a consequence of their decades of disobedience, they died in the wilderness rather than being allowed to enter the Promised Land.

With the transition from the exodus generation to the conquest generation, the spotlight shifts to two episodes from the early chapters of the book of Joshua: the fall of Jericho and the salvation of Rahab. In a stunning contrast, the author of Hebrews pairs Israel's corporate faith under the godly leader Joshua, embodied in the seven-day ritual encircling the city, with the personal faith of a Canaanite prostitute. These twin narratives, drawn from Joshua 2 and 6, showcase that faith is not bound by ethnicity, morality, or status but only by response to God's Word. The big idea is that what truly matters most is faith in the God of the Bible.

Joshua's Faith

The conquest of Jericho, Israel's first major engagement in Canaan, is narrated in Joshua 6. Jericho was a fortified city, and the strategy God gave Joshua defied all conventional military logic: for six days the people were to march silently around the city, followed by a final day of seven circuits and a trumpet blast. The fortified military city walls collapsed, not by human siege, but by divine intervention. Behind this act of obedience was trust in God's promise of victory.

Joshua, whose name means "the LORD saves" in Hebrew, was a significant figure in ancient Israelite history, with his name appearing a few hundred times in the Bible. Originally named Hoshea, he was renamed Joshua by Moses[a] and served as his successor, leading the Israelites in their conquest of Canaan. Joshua played crucial roles during the Exodus, including proving to be a skilled warrior, leading a successful battle against the Amalekites[b], and serving as Moses' assistant in the tent of meeting.[c] As one of the 12 spies sent to explore Canaan, Joshua, along with Caleb, gave a favorable report and encouraged the Israelites to have faith in God. God appointed Joshua to succeed Moses, and he was commissioned to lead the people into the Promised Land. The book of Joshua details his leadership in conquering Canaan and distributing the land among the tribes of Israel. Joshua is remembered for his faith, obedience to God, and effective leadership. He lived to be 110 years old and was buried in his allotted territory, which has now been unearthed and confirmed by archaeologists.[32]

Joshua's faith sustained him through two of the greatest moves of God in the Bible. One, he was at the side of Moses, helping lead the Exodus from Egypt. Two, some 40 years later, he replaced Moses and led God's people into the Promised Land in fulfillment of God's promise to Abraham and Sarah over 600 years prior. Joshua's faith is revealed as strength and courage in God's promises, despite all circumstances seeming contrary and impossible. Deuteronomy 31:7–8 famously says,

> Then Moses summoned Joshua and said to him in the sight of all Israel, "Be strong and courageous, for you shall go with this people into the land that the LORD has sworn to their fathers to give them, and you shall put them in possession of it. It is the LORD who goes before you. He will be with you; he will not leave you or forsake you. Do not fear or be dismayed."

Joshua's faith, and ours, is in a faithful God.

---

[a] Numbers 13:16 [b] Exodus 17:8-13 [c] Exodus 33:11

In Joshua 8, his faith is on display when he built an altar as the people watched, obeying the commands of Moses.[a] Today, it is common for people to have a private faith, but with Joshua, his faith was entirely public. As a leader, he was setting a public example of worshipful obedience to God's commands for everyone else to follow.

As one of the 12 spies, he and Caleb were in the minority with enough faith to trust that the land belonged to God and that God would displace their enemies and give it to them.[b] For this faith, the men were exempt from the generation sentenced to die in the wilderness as judgment, permitting them to lead God's people into the land promised in the Abrahamic Covenant.

In one of the Bible's more famous miracle scenes[c], Joshua asked that the Lord would divinely intervene, thereby providing more time for their battle against the Amorites. Joshua 10:12-14 says,

> At that time Joshua spoke to the Lord in the day when the Lord gave the Amorites over to the sons of Israel, and he said in the sight of Israel, "Sun, stand still at Gibeon, and moon, in the Valley of Aijalon." And the sun stood still, and the moon stopped, until the nation took vengeance on their enemies…The sun stopped in the midst of heaven and did not hurry to set for about a whole day. There has been no day like it before or since, when the Lord heeded the voice of a man, for the Lord fought for Israel.

Over and over, God shows up in power, answering the prayers of Joshua. It's abundantly clear that God is the hero, but the requests that Joshua makes of God reveal an incredible faith in the unlimited supernatural power of God.

Unlike some people who do not finish their race well, the closing scenes from Joshua's life reveal a man of tremendous, seasoned, and unwavering faith in his last days. Before dying, it

---

[a] Deuteronomy 27 [b] Numbers 14:6-10 [c] Joshua 10

is reported in Joshua 23 that he assembled the various leaders of the nation and gave testimony of God's faithfulness and commanded them to live in faith, saying,

> "I am now old and well advanced in years. And you have seen all that the Lord your God has done to all these nations for your sake, for it is the Lord your God who has fought for you…The Lord your God will push them back before you and drive them out of your sight. And you shall possess their land, just as the Lord your God promised you. Therefore, be very strong to keep and to do all that is written in the Book of the Law of Moses, turning aside from it neither to the right hand nor to the left, that you may not mix with these nations remaining among you or make mention of the names of their gods or swear by them or serve them or bow down to them, but you shall cling to the Lord your God just as you have done to this day. For the Lord has driven out before you great and strong nations. And as for you, no man has been able to stand before you to this day. One man of you puts to flight a thousand, since it is the Lord your God who fights for you, just as he promised you. Be very careful, therefore, to love the Lord your God. For if you turn back and cling to the remnant of these nations remaining among you and make marriages with them, so that you associate with them and they with you, know for certain that the Lord your God will no longer drive out these nations before you, but they shall be a snare and a trap for you, a whip on your sides and thorns in your eyes, until you perish from off this good ground that the Lord your God has given you. And now I am about to go the way of all the earth, and you know in your hearts and souls, all of you, that not one word has failed of all the good things that the Lord your God promised concerning you. All have come to pass for you; not one of them has failed. But just as all the good things that the Lord your God promised concerning you have been fulfilled for you, so the Lord will bring upon you all the evil things, until he has destroyed

you from off this good land that the Lord your God has given you, if you transgress the covenant of the Lord your God, which he commanded you, and go and serve other gods and bow down to them. Then the anger of the Lord will be kindled against you, and you shall perish quickly from off the good land that he has given to you."[a]

Before dying, Joshua then preached a sermon[b] reminding everyone of the faithfulness of God all the way back to the saving and sending of Abraham over 600 years prior. In that sermon, he also teaches them about the God of Abraham, Isaac, and Jacob; demonic attacks from false "gods"; Moses and Aaron; the Exodus deliverance and parting of the Red Sea; numerous wars the Lord had given victory in through many generations; and he reminds them of God's Word delivered through the prophets. In a closing scene that is reminiscent of an old-school Billy Graham revival crusade, Joshua preaches for a decision:

> "Now therefore fear the Lord and serve him in sincerity and in faithfulness. Put away the gods that your fathers served...and serve the Lord. And if it is evil in your eyes to serve the Lord, choose this day whom you will serve...But as for me and my house, we will serve the Lord."[c]

The people were so moved by Joshua's faith that they, too, responded in faith, promising in a sacred covenant to "also... serve the Lord, for he is our God."[d] Joshua then warned the people of the solemn vow they were making, starting with the men deciding for their families, because God is "holy" and "jealous."[e] It is reported,

> And the people said to Joshua, "No, but we will serve the Lord." Then Joshua said to the people, "You are witnesses against yourselves that you have chosen the Lord, to serve him." And they said, "We are witnesses."

[a] Joshua 23:2, 3, 5-16 [b] Joshua 24 [c] Joshua 24:14-15 [d] Joshua 24:18 [e] Joshua 24:19

He said, "Then put away the foreign gods that are among you, and incline your heart to the Lord, the God of Israel." And the people said to Joshua, "The Lord our God we will serve, and his voice we will obey." So Joshua made a covenant with the people that day, and put in place statutes and rules for them at Shechem. And Joshua wrote these words in the Book of the Law of God. And he took a large stone and set it up there under the terebinth that was by the sanctuary of the Lord. And Joshua said to all the people, "Behold, this stone shall be a witness against us, for it has heard all the words of the Lord that he spoke to us. Therefore it shall be a witness against you, lest you deal falsely with your God." So Joshua sent the people away...[a]

Joshua then died and was buried at the age of 110. The people who were led and taught by Joshua remained faithful to the Lord after his death, as Joshua 24:31 reports: "Israel served the Lord all the days of Joshua, and all the days of the elders who outlived Joshua and had known all the work that the Lord did for Israel."

Joshua's faith led to a legacy of faith for an entire generation of a nation following his death. Despite being one of the greatest men who ever lived, Joshua also needed the grace of God for the few days he experienced failure instead of faith.

Joshua's Failure

Although Joshua is not a perfect man, he is one of the greatest men to walk the earth. He humbly serves under the leadership of Moses and is one of the few who God did not decree to die in the wilderness between Egypt and Israel, instead choosing him to be the leader of a new nation. Joshua is an incredible man of God with consistent faith that grows throughout his life. He is a history-changing leader, worshiper, preacher, and warrior. In comparison to other people mentioned

[a] Joshua 24:21-28

in Hebrews 11, Joshua's life has few occasions reported in the Scriptures where he sinned against God.

First, God told Joshua he had been praying too long and needed to get up and go deal with a wicked man named Achan, who was largely responsible for their military defeat due to his sinfulness of stealing.[a] God's people had just suffered a disastrous defeat at the little city of Ai just after a great victory at the much bigger city of Jericho. God allowed victory for obedience, and He allowed this defeat due to Achan's disobedience. It appears that Joshua and his advisers did not seek the Lord's battle plan for Ai, which caused the loss of the battle and took the lives of 36 men. As the leader, it was Joshua's job to ensure that he received God's battle plan in prayer and to be aware of any gross sin in the troops he was leading. Joshua's response to spend extended time face down in humble, repentant prayer was good and noble, but God told him to also get up and fix the problem by dealing with the sin of Achan. The moral of the story is that sometimes you need to pray a short prayer, get up, take responsibility, fight evil, and answer that prayer yourself.

Secondly, the only other mention of a notable failure or sin in Joshua's life is found in Joshua 9. The man of God again failed to prayerfully ask the Lord's guidance. After the battles of Jericho and Ai, the Gibeonites saw their end was drawing near, so they put on quite a theatrical display to deceive and dupe Joshua and his soldiers. They pretended to have travelled from a far-away country, complete with moldy bread, worn-out clothes and shoes, and an old sack to carry goods on their donkeys. They pretended to have interest in the God of Joshua and asked to make a pact to live in peace. Three short days later, it was revealed that the Gibeonites were actually lying Canaanites from nations God had commanded His people to utterly destroy. However, because Joshua vowed peace, he said, "We have sworn to them by the LORD, the God of Israel, and now we may not touch them."[b] The fact that Joshua served the Lord in Egypt, the wilderness, and the Promised Land over the

---

[a] Joshua 7:10-15 [b] Joshua 9:19

course of his 110 years, warring in battles and worshiping at every step, his failures are quite minor in comparison to other leaders mentioned in Hebrews 11, including Samson, who drank, gambled, murdered, tortured animals, and slept with prostitutes, and whom we will study in an upcoming chapter.

Our Faithful God

In His sovereignty, God chose Joshua as a leader and filled him with the Holy Spirit to do the job. Numbers 27:18–23 says,

> So the Lord said to Moses, "Take Joshua…a man in whom is the Spirit, and lay your hand on him. Make him stand before Eleazar the priest and all the congregation, and you shall commission him in their sight. You shall invest him with some of your authority, that all the congregation of the people of Israel may obey. And he shall stand before Eleazar the priest, who shall inquire for him by the judgment…before the Lord. At his word they shall go out, and at his word they shall come in, both he and all the people of Israel with him, the whole congregation." And Moses did as the Lord commanded him. He took Joshua and made him stand before Eleazar the priest and the whole congregation, and he laid his hands on him and commissioned him as the Lord directed through Moses.

God's faithfulness to Joshua included a divine visit. God sent from Heaven to Earth the "commander of the army of the Lord."[a] In response, "Joshua fell on his face…and worshiped," calling this divine being "my lord." Like when Moses met with Jesus at the burning bush (Exodus 3:5), Joshua 5:15 reports that Joshua was told, "'Take off your sandals from your feet, for the place where you are standing is holy.' And Joshua did so." In this scene, we witness how intimately involved God is in leading Joshua and establishing His divine authority over the

[a] Joshua 5:13-15

man who was over the nation.

    God also showed up in power to do the impossible. God famously caused the walls of Jericho to fall under Joshua's leadership, as reported in Joshua 6 and confirmed by archaeological digs.[33] While God's people were away from the Promised Land for more than 400 years, as expected, their enemies had moved in, fortified their cities with walls, and had no intention of vacating what had been their home for generations. Conversely, God's people sought to claim what was assigned to them by God in the Abrahamic Covenant. The first city to be conquered in Canaan by Joshua's army was the military stronghold at Jericho. In what would require incredible humility and faith to believe and leadership to execute, God instructed the spiritual leaders (priests) to silently march around the impenetrable fortified military walls with three things: the ark of the Lord housing the 10 Commandments God wrote for Moses, a pot of manna from the wilderness wanderings in Exodus, and Aaron's rod through which God did many miracles to judge Egypt and deliver His people. Each of these was a sacred reminder of God's presence and power. On the seventh day, the process was repeated seven times, and, in faith, on the final lap, the people shouted, and God powerfully tore down the walls before them! This was an incredibly overwhelming show of God's power in response to faith-filled obedience. One can only imagine the mockery His worshipers experienced from their enemies...until God got the last laugh. Joshua obeyed God, leading the victorious nation to kill everyone except Rahab and her household, who had served the Lord[a], and take precious metals as spoils of war, adding them to the Lord's treasury.

    In faith, Joshua led an army in battle once again.[b] However, their victory was because of God's divine intervention: "And the LORD said to Joshua, 'Do not be afraid of them, for tomorrow at this time I will give over all of them, slain, to Israel'...And the LORD gave them into the hand of Israel... And Joshua did to them just as the LORD said to him..."[c]

---

[a] Joshua 2 [b] Joshua 11 [c] Joshua 11:6, 8, 9

Over and over, God speaks, Joshua has faith, and he acts in obedience, trusting God to do as He promises, which He always does. Furthermore, in faith, Joshua also obeys the Word of God written down by Moses, believing that God will bless obedience to the Scriptures. Joshua 11 reports repeatedly that Joshua did "just as Moses the servant of the LORD had commanded... Just as the LORD had commanded Moses his servant, so Moses commanded Joshua, and so Joshua did. He left nothing undone of all that the LORD had commanded Moses."[a]

God was faithful when Joshua had faith in His Word. That simple lesson is the reason Joshua was a great man of God and the key lesson for anyone to learn who wants to live by faith.

Dig Deeper.

1. To learn more about Joshua, read Joshua 1-6, which covers Israel's preparations, crossing the Jordan, and the fall of Jericho; 7-12, which describes the major military campaigns; and 22-24, containing Joshua's farewells.

Walk it out. Talk it out.

1. What most surprised you about Joshua's faith and failure? Why?
2. What did the Holy Spirit highlight for you as you studied the life of Joshua?
3. What are some of the most memorable ways God has proven Himself faithful in your life?
4. How can group members be praying for each other this week?

---

[a] Joshua 11:12, 15

HEBREWS 11

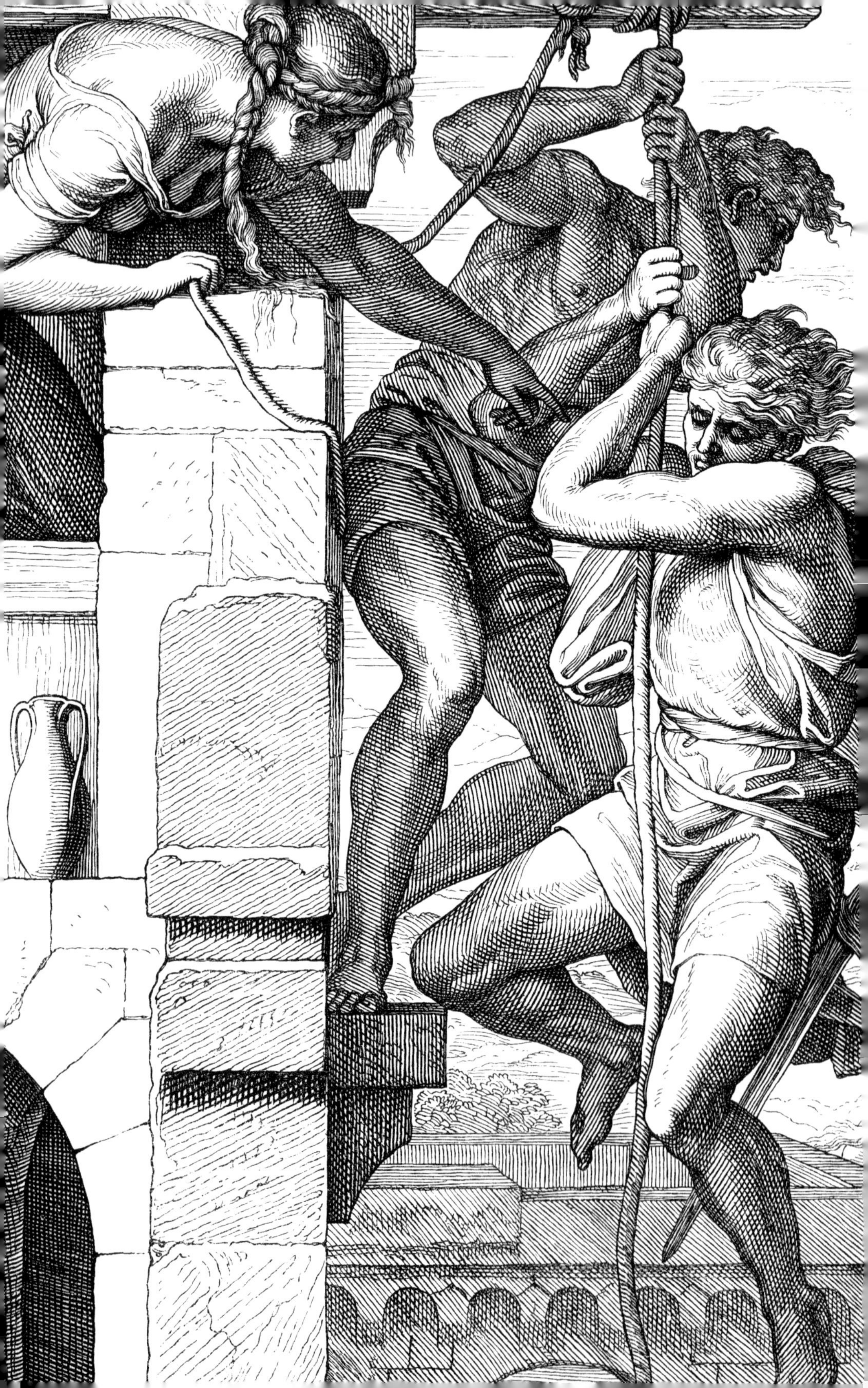

RAHAB

Chapter 11: Faith for Rahab
Hebrews 11:31

Hebrews 11:31 – By faith Rahab the prostitute did not perish with those who were disobedient, because she had given a friendly welcome to the spies.

Rahab enters the storyline of the Bible when her life intersects with Joshua. After the generation of Moses died in the wilderness because of their rebellion against God, Joshua and Caleb were permitted to lead the next generation to take the Promised Land given by God to the Hebrews in the Abrahamic Covenant over 600 years prior. Having left Egypt by God's deliverance, and after spending 40 years wandering in the wilderness, the time had come for the land to belong to God's people, setting up what would become the nation of Israel, the Temple, the sacrificial system, the remaining Scriptures through the Hebrew prophets, and the coming of Jesus Christ. All of human history was hinging on Joshua taking the land, in faith, by God's help, occupied by fierce enemies.

Rahab's Faith

As a wise military strategist, Joshua sent two spies to investigate the land, especially the military stronghold city of Jericho, fortified with secure walls. Needing lodging, the military spies doing reconnaissance on their enemy found lodging at one of the most outcast and private places possible—the home of a prostitute named Rahab.[a]

> "I know that the Lord has given you the land, and that the fear of you has fallen upon us, and that all the inhabitants of the land melt away before you. For we have heard how the Lord dried up the water of the Red Sea before you when you came out of Egypt, and what you did to the two kings of the Amorites who were beyond the

[a] Joshua 2

Jordan, to Sihon and Og, whom you devoted to destruction. And as soon as we heard it, our hearts melted, and there was no spirit left in any man because of you, for the Lord your God, he is God in the heavens above and on the earth beneath."[a]

This is Rahab converting to the worship of the God of Israel, standing against her own nation and people. Furthermore, a Biblical archaeology journal says,

> Rahab knows that "Yahweh your God is God in heaven above and on the earth below." The phrase "God in heaven above" is used by only three biblical figures: Moses, Solomon and Rahab. What a combination! The phrase "Yahweh your God is God" is also unusual. It appears only three other times in the Hebrew Bible…(Jeremiah 10:10; 2 Chronicles 20:6, Psalm 100:3)… After pledging her allegiance to the God she just converted to, Rahab then presses the spies to pledge themselves to her and her family's safety, insisting that they swear "by Yahweh" (Joshua 2:12).[34]

It goes on to say,

> These very words are invariably spoken by Israelites and their ancestors starting with Abraham in Genesis 24:3… Rahab's confession of faith results in her being spared by Joshua and accepted into the house of Israel. "Her family has lived in Israel ever since. For she hid the messengers whom Joshua sent to spy out Jericho" (Joshua 6:25). In a remarkable reversal, the quintessential Canaanite, whose very occupation epitomized Canaanitism from the Israelite perspective, has become an Israelite.[35]

Rahab would have been considered perhaps the least likely candidate to help God's people accomplish their divine mission

[a] Joshua 2:9-11

for at least two reasons.

One, Rahab is a Canaanite. Today, some of their descendants are the Palestinians living in the Gaza Strip, which is in conflict with Israel 3000 years later as the battle between their descendants continues. This collection of various ancient tribes mentioned in the Old Testament (e.g., Phoenicians, Philistines, Hittites) were the most detested enemies of God and His people. They were well-known for being extremely morally depraved and sexually disgusting, with gross perversion of every sort celebrated publicly without shame. A Bible handbook says,

> The nations of Canaan were known to be the most sexually perverted, morally depraved, and bloodthirsty peoples of all ancient history. Their depravity is mentioned in the Bible (Gen. 13:13; 15:16; 18:20; 19:1–11; Num. 25:1–3; Judg. 19:14–25; 1 Kings 14:24; 15:12; 22:46; 2 Kings 23:7). It is also mentioned by Philo of Byblos, a Phoenician scholar c. 100 b.c., and in the literature of ancient Ugarit… It was because of the depravity of the Canaanites that God gave their land back to the Jews and ordered their extermination (Deut. 7:1–5; 20:10–15; Josh. 9:24).[36]

By the time of Joshua, God commanded that the Canaanite people be forever removed because they were the greatest threat to seducing His people into sin, especially sexual sin. In Deuteronomy 7:1–5, God commanded,

> When the Lord your God brings you into the land that you are entering to take possession of it, and clears away many nations before you…the Canaanites…and when the Lord your God gives them over to you, and you defeat them, then you must devote them to complete destruction. You shall make no covenant with them and show no mercy to them. You shall not intermarry with them, giving your daughters to their sons or taking their daughters for your sons, for they would turn away your sons from following me, to serve other gods. Then the anger of the Lord would

be kindled against you, and he would destroy you quickly. But thus shall you deal with them: you shall break down their altars and dash in pieces their pillars and chop down their Asherim and burn their carved images with fire.

The reclaiming of the land by God's people and orders to depose or destroy the Canaanites was God's way of conquering their demon gods and protecting His people from falling into gross sin.

The failure to completely remove these demonic and disgusting people leads to the days of the Judges, which we will study next, as God's people joined in their corruption and, in green, made them slaves to profit from them. Judges 1:27–28 reports of God's people, "…[they] did not drive out the inhabitants…the Canaanites persisted in dwelling in that land. When Israel grew strong, they put the Canaanites to forced labor, but did not drive them out completely." Judges 3:5–8 later reports that

> the people of Israel lived among the Canaanites…And their daughters they took to themselves for wives, and their own daughters they gave to their sons, and they served their gods. And the people did…evil in the sight of the LORD. They forgot the LORD their God and served the Baals and the Asheroth. Therefore the anger of the LORD was kindled…

The remainder of Judges reports how one generation after the next is more compromised by the Canaanites, with King Ahab and Queen Jezebel rising as the literal human embodiment of the demons Baal and Asherah.

Two, Rahab is a prostitute. A Bible Handbook says,

> In Canaanite religions temple prostitutes had intercourse with the worshipers in order to make sure that their fields and flocks would be fertile…that temple prostitution was a problem in Israel.…Such a person was found in Canaanite temples, where fertility gods were worshiped. It was

believed that intercourse with such a prostitute would make fields and herds fertile.[37]

Canaanite prostitution was demonic, with brothels serving as shrines where demons were worshiped in hopes of getting financial favor from a bountiful crop harvest. Despite being forbidden, temple prostitution became a recurring problem in ancient Israel, which is why the prophets throughout the Old Testament keep commanding it to stop (Hosea 4:13-14; Amos 2:7; Jeremiah 2:20, 3:6-10; Ezekiel 16:15-22, 23:37-39; Deuteronomy 22:21, 23:17-18; 1 Kings 14:24, 15:12; 2 Kings 21:6, 23:7, 23:4-7; Leviticus 19:29; Micah 1:7; Nahum 3:4).[38&39]

Bible scholars suggest that the story of Rahab has been overly sanitized:

> Perhaps not surprisingly, the biblical narrative describing this encounter with the prostitute is redolent with sexual innuendo. But, as we shall see, the bawdy allusions do not simply re-create the atmosphere found in this house of prostitution. Nor are the allusions only crude attempts to spice up the plot. Instead, they help strengthen Rahab's identity with Canaan and underscore the greatest threat Canaan presents to Israel: idol worship, or in biblical terms, "whoring after idols."…Rahab's house…in which the spies seek overnight accommodations, is hardly a private home. This is a house of ill-repute…Rahab was…a prostitute. As head of the household, she may actually have been a madam. The reference to the two men "spending the night" in Rahab's establishment is almost certainly a *double entendre*…[and sometimes] means "to sleep with," "to be sexually intimate," as in Genesis 19:32–35, in which each of Lot's daughters "lies…with her father."[40&41]

The first readers of Hebrews 11 would have been shocked to see a Canaanite prostitute on the list of exemplary believers. However, it is a wonderful reminder that our God saves by grace alone, through faith alone, which is why He receives the glory alone!

Rahab's Failure

Rahab's life starts as badly as one could imagine. She is explicitly identified as "Rahab the prostitute." Furthermore, as a Canaanite, Rahab belonged to a people marked for destruction due to their pervasive wickedness.[a] Despite the profound failures in her early life, once she becomes a believer in and follower of the One True God, her life forever changes.

Although Rahab had not seen God act in miraculous might, she trusted the report of God's power. Importantly, Rahab never saw God show up in power, and He never spoke to her. Her faith rested solely in the report of God's power, which she believed by faith. Furthermore, her heart immediately opened to the Lord when she converted on the same day that she met believers in the God of Israel for the first time in her life. Her faith is great and far greater than most Christians today. In Joshua 2:9-12, she says,

> "I know that the Lord has given you the land, and that the fear of you has fallen upon us...For we have heard how the Lord dried up the water of the Red Sea before you when you came out of Egypt, and what you did to the two kings of the Amorites who were beyond the Jordan, to Sihon and Og, whom you devoted to destruction. And as soon as we heard it, our hearts melted, and there was no spirit left in any man because of you, for the Lord your God, he is God in the heavens above and on the earth beneath. Now then, please swear to me by the Lord that, as I have dealt kindly with you, you also will deal kindly with my father's house..."

Unlike so many believers in the Bible, including in Hebrews 11, who did not finish their life walking faithfully

---
[a] Deut 9:4-5

with God, there is no report that she did the same. This is because Rahab's faith, despite her previous failure, was in a faithful God. She is a wonderful story of a sinful, broken, demonic woman who was radically saved by God, fully devoted to Him, and never looked back.

Our Faithful God

Not only is Rahab spared by God. We read in Joshua 6:16–17,

> Joshua said to the people, "Shout, for the Lord has given you the city. And the city and all that is within it shall be devoted to the Lord for destruction. Only Rahab the prostitute and all who are with her in her house shall live, because she hid the messengers whom we sent."

Unlike the rest of those living in the mighty city of Jericho, Rahab and her family were spared because of her faith in God and serving God's people. She is literally one-of-a-kind.

Not only was Rahab spared by God, but she was also profoundly blessed and honored by God. There are four Gospels that tell the testimony of Jesus Christ—Matthew, Mark, Luke, and John—and the first is written by a Jewish man, firstly intended to be read by Jewish people. This explains why Matthew begins his book with the genealogy of Jesus Christ, tracing Him back to Abraham, the Jewish people, and what they considered the purer family history compared to other godless, pagan nations. Matthew 1 begins, "...the genealogy of Jesus Christ, the son of David, the son of Abraham. Abraham was the father of Isaac, and Isaac the father of Jacob, and Jacob the father of Judah and his brothers..." Until this point, the original readers would not have been shocked, and then everything changes with who appears next in the genealogy of Jesus Christ: "and Salmon the father of Boaz by Rahab, and Boaz the father of Obed by Ruth, and Obed the father of Jesse, and Jesse the father of David the king."

In a rather shocking report to ancient readers, the inclusion of four women in Jesus' genealogy is very unexpected and, to some, even scandalous. A Bible commentary says,

> A number of women figure in the genealogy. That might not seem strange in today's climate, but it was startling in a Jewish genealogy. In both Greek and Jewish culture a woman had no legal rights. She could not inherit property or give testimony in a court of law. She was completely under her husband's power. She was seen less as a person than as a thing. The Jewish man thanked God each day that he had not been created a slave, a Gentile or a woman. And yet here are four women in Jesus' genealogy. And what women! *Tamar* was an adulteress [Genesis 38]. *Rahab* was a prostitute from pagan Jericho [Joshua 2:1-7]. *Uriah's wife*, Bathsheba, was the woman David had seduced and whose first child had died, but through whose subsequent son Solomon the royal line was traced [2 Samuel 11-12]. *Ruth* was not even a Jewess at all, but a Moabitess [Ruth 1:4], and Moabites and their descendants were not allowed near the assembly of the Lord [Deuteronomy 23:3]. These are the women introduced into the genealogy to prepare us for the climax of them all—*Mary*! Matthew could not have found a more amazing selection of women wherever he had looked within the pages of his Bible.[42]

Rahab is not merely spared—she is incorporated into the lineage of Israel and, ultimately, the Messianic line leading to Jesus Christ.[a] Her story prefigures the inclusion of Gentiles into the people of God through faith long before Paul would expound it. That she "did not perish with those who were disobedient"[b] underscores the two options that Hebrews repeatedly gives: faith saves; disobedience destroys. In the life of Rahab, God receives the glory for both the fall of a mighty city and the salvation of a marginal woman. The same God who judges Jericho redeems Rahab. He exalts the lowly and humbles

---

[a] Matthew 1:5 [b] Hebrews 11:31

the haughty. A Bible commentator notes, "God's saving activity was already operative in the most unlikely of people, in the most unexpected of places."[43]

Jesus Christ is a global God and Savior. He saves those who repent of sin and trust in Him from any nation, in any generation. The inclusion of Rahab in the family line of Jesus makes the point that salvation is by grace alone through faith alone abundantly clear. A Bible commentary says, "Matthew is surely saying that the gospel is for all people, not Jews only, and that the gospel is for sinners. It is a sinful world, and Matthew is writing about grace."[44]

Jesus' half-brother James also honored the repentant faith of Rahab. James 2:24-25 says, "You see that a person is justified by works and not by faith alone. And in the same way was not also Rahab the prostitute justified by works when she received the messengers and sent them out by another way?" In this Scripture, James portrays Rahab as a model of faith, with her actions being evidence of her complete trust in God despite the risks to her own life and family.

Throughout Jewish and Christian history, Rahab has remained a very popular person because of her testimony that repentance and faith change everything. While we cannot be sure about her later life, because the Scriptures are silent, there are some curious reports.

> According to later Jewish legend, Rahab was one of the four most beautiful women in history. She became a righteous convert, married Joshua, and was the ancestor of eight prophets (including Jeremiah) and Huldah the prophetess. In the NT [NEW TESTAMENT], Rahab is cited as a heroine of faith (Heb. 11:31) and of righteous works (James 2:25). She is listed in the ancestry of Jesus in Matthew's Gospel, which also indicates that she married Joshua (1:5).[45]

Whatever the case, Rahab should encourage us that no one is beyond the grace of God, and, sometimes, the people with the worst sin have the strongest faith once they meet Jesus

HEBREWS 11

Christ as God and Savior!

Dig Deeper.
1. To learn more about Joshua and Rahab, read Joshua 2.

Walk it out. Talk it out.
1. What most surprises you about Rahab's faith and failure? Why?
2. Take some time as a group discussing how the grace and mercy of God is on full display in the saving of Rahab and her family. How encouraging is her story to those who have an awful past?
3. In the stories of Joshua and Rahab, including other people involved, what are the big 1-2 lessons God had for you?
4. How can group members be praying for each other this week?

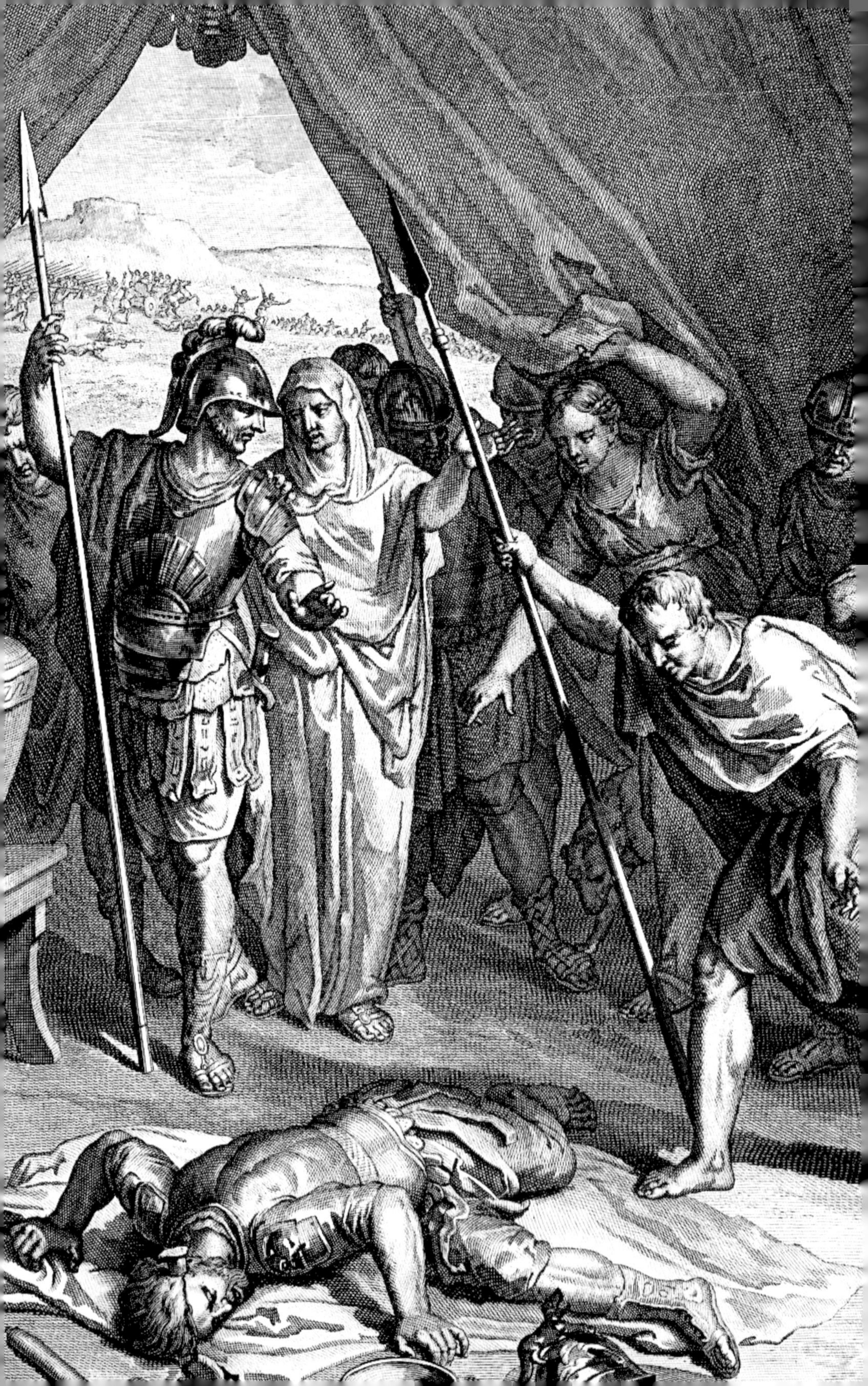

BARAK

Chapter 12: Faith for Barak
Hebrews 11:32

Hebrews 11:32 – And what more shall I say? For time would fail me to tell of Gideon, Barak, Samson, Jephthah…

Consider a nation in steep spiritual and cultural decline—lacking godly and strong leadership, surrounded by major shifts in political relationships with other nations, and during a time of economic change causing internal social unrest, division, rioting, and terrorism leading to anarchy and a complete disregard for God and the rule of law.

While this backdrop sounds much like our day, it is also the setting for the time written about in Judges, which reports a significant season of transition for God's people in the Old Testament. They needed leadership, as the time had not come for a king, so the judges were interim leaders both politically and spiritually.

The first judge God raised up was Moses. Exodus 18:13 says, "Moses sat to judge the people…."

Hebrews 11:32 lists four of the judges—Barak, Gideon, Samson, and Jephthah. We will study them in the order that they appear historically. That period of history was incredibly dark, as God's people were rebellious and defiant for generations. God commanded His people in Deuteronomy 12:8, "You shall not do according to all that we are doing here today, everyone doing whatever is right in his own eyes…" The last line of Judges[a] echoes this and is the summary of this evil season, saying, "Everyone did what was right in his own eyes."

The first five books of the Bible are the "law," with 613 commands given by God. Judges reports how God's people violated many of those laws, especially those in the book of Deuteronomy. God commanded His people to drive the pagans out of the land, but instead they enslaved and kept them.[b] God commanded His people to destroy the demonic Canaanite places of worship, and an angel rebukes the people for not

[a] Judges 21:25 [b] Deut 7:2; Judges 1:3-36

doing so.ᵃ God commanded parents to evangelize and disciple their own children to become believers, but an entire generation grew up not knowing God.ᵇ God commanded His people to not marry the demonic Canaanites, but they angered God by doing this very thing.ᶜ The book of Judges repeatedly mentions the sins of the people.ᵈ They would defy God, and He would allow pain to occur as discipline to get them to repent and change course, but they would proceed further into sin with even greater pain. A Bible dictionary says,

> This fall back into bondage is a leading motif in the history that follows. We see the cycle in Judges, where in response to Israel's sin, the Lord repeatedly "sold them into the power of their enemies round about" (Judg 2:14; cf. 3:7, 12; 4:2; 6:1; 10:7; 13:1). The process reaches a climax in 2 Kings 17, when Israel is finally deported to political bondage in Assyria.⁴⁶

The story of Judges is this: when we do not walk with God, we walk into trouble, and our family and friends follow into tragedy. Comfort and ease cause people to wander from God. Furthermore, Satan runs the world and seduces God's people into sin. Throughout Judges, God's people continually wander into the worship of the demonic false god Baal and follow the sexual and spiritual practices of the nearby ungodly Canaanites. Powerful demonic spirits work through everything and anything from religion to spirituality, politics, education, and entertainment to lure people away from pure devotion to the One True God. These powerful demonic forces are referred to as a "god" or the "gods" throughout Judges.ᵉ Demon spirits parading as false gods work together under Baal, the chief god of the Canaanite legion. His name is translated with terms like "master," "lord," and "owner." Judges speaks of both Baalᶠ and Baals.ᵍ Like any military fighting unit with human beings,

---

ᵃ Deut 12:3; Judges 2:1-6 ᵇ Deut 6:6-7; Judges 2:7-12 ᶜ Deut 7:3-4; Judges 3:5-8 ᵈ Judges 2:11; 3:7-8, 12; 4:1; 6:1; 10:6; 13:1 ᵉ 2:3, 2:12, 2:17, 2:19, 3:6, 5:8, 6:10, 6:31, 8:33, 9:9, 9:27, 10:6, 10:13-14, 10:16, 11:24, 16:23-24, 17:5, 18:14, 18:17-18, 18:20, 18:24 ᶠ 6:25, 6:28, 6:30, 6:31, 6:32 ᵍ 2:11, 2:13, 3:3, 3:7, 6:25, 8:33, 9:4, 10:6, 10:10, 20:33

demonic divine beings in the unseen realm also have a chain of command. At the top is the demon "Baal," and working under that demon are the various demon "Baals." Although demons are not male or female with a physical body like human beings, Baal appears as a male demonic deity.

Baal was considered the most powerful demonic deity and god of wealth, prosperity, and success. Throughout Judges, Baal is also often mentioned as working with Ashtaroth or Asherah.[a] This demon appeared as a female and the goddess of fertility and sex. Also known as Venus, she was the highest-ranking Canaanite demonic goddess and was considered the passionate lover of Baal. The worship of Baal and Ashtaroth included sex without any limits, pleasure and indulgence of every kind, and even child sacrifice. God's people kept falling back into this sin, and the pattern continues to this day with the constant lure of wealth, power, success, pleasure, comfort, sex, indulgence, and pornography. Our new days have the same old demons.

A Bible commentary says,

> Judges also contributes to the understanding of how contemporary culture and other religions can bring immense pressure upon the people of God. The battle is with the world system that pressures believers, successfully at times, to reject God. The book of Judges emphasizes that a key problem for Israel was forgetting God's great acts of the past, especially the Exodus from Egypt. The Passover and all of Israel's feasts were designed to keep the people remembering God's great redemptive acts. When they forgot what God had done in the past, they inevitably excluded God from their present.[47]

The sad, hard truth is we are often our own worst enemy. Throughout the book of Judges, the people truly have no one to blame for their hardships other than themselves. If we are honest, the same is often true of us. We have all made choices that have caused pain in our own lives. Much of this comes

---

[a] 2:13, 3:7, 6:25-30, 10:6

from being impulsive, chasing pleasure or comfort, or becoming bored with life and ungrateful to God. This is the backdrop of Judges.

Everything rises or falls with leadership. Throughout the book of Judges, when there are godly leaders, things get better for a season, and when there are ungodly leaders, things get worse. For the most part, God's people throughout Judges struggle to produce good leaders, and their one attempt at a king was a disaster. Judges painfully illustrates the need for godly, Spirit-led leadership, as cultures decline and people fail without it.

Barak's Faith

Curiously, the list of those with faith in Hebrews 11 mentions Barak but not his boss, Deborah. Wrongly often portrayed as a feminist, Deborah was indeed not a feminist. In fact, she rejoiced when men led. In Judges 5:2 (NIV), Deborah says, "When the princes in Israel take the lead, when the people willingly offer themselves—praise the Lord!"

Deborah stepped up to lead in one of the darkest hours in the Old Testament. A Bible dictionary says, "Deborah judged Israel after Shamgar. When Deborah was raised as a judge, Israel had been oppressed by King Jabin of Canaan for 20 years (Judg 4:2–3)."[48]

The days of Judges were filled with ungodly men not leading as God commanded. So, God worked through a godly, obedient woman rather than ungodly, disobedient men. Deborah stepped up like a single mother does or as a vice president does when the president is gone. Deborah was strong, but she was not independent. She continually works closely with and through godly men, including Barak. Deborah was a Spirit-filled woman of God who would get leadership directives from the Lord and then communicate them to Barak, who would lead the male soldiers into war. In Judges 4, this is precisely what happens. Barak, not Deborah, is honored for his battlefield heroics in 1 Samuel 12:11: "…the Lord sent Jerubbaal and Barak and Jephthah and Samuel and delivered you out of the hand of your enemies on every side, and you lived in safety."

Barak's faith is on full display in Judges 5. There, it is Barak and Deborah, political and military leaders, who lead God's people to sing in worship to Him, praising Him for their victory. The chapter begins, "Then sang Deborah and Barak…: 'That the leaders took the lead in Israel, that the people offered themselves willingly, bless the Lord! Hear, O kings; give ear, O princes; to the Lord I will sing; I will make melody to the Lord, the God of Israel.'"

Barak's Failure

While Barak does not appear as the most courageous of leaders, perhaps his faith is noteworthy because he was one of the godliest men during the darkest of days. The days of the Judges lacked nearly anyone with integrity, especially the men. In comparison to other men, Barak was a giant of the faith.

Knowing God's time for war had come, Judges 4:6 says Deborah "summoned Barak…and said to him, 'Has not the LORD, the God of Israel, commanded you…'" Barak is a bit of a timid man who knows God has called him to lead the men into battle, but he's not yet activated on that calling. Deborah demonstrates more courage, reminding him of their battle plan, but he weakly says, "If you will go with me, I will go, but if you will not go with me, I will not go."[a] If you can imagine a high-ranking military general refusing to go into war unless a female political or judicial leader rode into battle with him, then you rightly envision this silly scene. Like too many men, Barak struggles with insecurity, fear, and passivity. Conversely, Deborah agreed to go but rightly mocked him, saying his plan "will not lead to your glory, for the LORD will sell Sisera into the hand of a woman."[b]

Perhaps Barak wanted to have Deborah travel to the battle with him because God's anointing in the Spirit was upon her, which would bring the blessing on her to the place of war? If so,

[a] Judges 4:8 [b] Judges 4:9

Barak still does not look courageous in this scene, as God had already prophesied and promised victory, so he should not have feared. To be fair, Deborah did not enter the battle, as Barak did lead the fight with great success—the men killed enemy combatants in war and chased them down without retreat.

However, it is a Gentile woman who is honored as the most courageous combatant in the battle led by Barak and Deborah. Judges 4:16-22 and 5:24-27 report that the Canaanite commander Sisera fled for his life after being defeated and hid in the tent of Jael, who took a tent peg and hammered it through his head, ending his reign of terror. Judges 5:24 honors her, saying, "Most blessed of women be Jael…" Despite being women, Deborah and Jael often demonstrate stronger courage and faith than Barak. He does obey God and leads men into battle but also struggles with confidence, like many believers.

<u>Our Faithful God</u>

Barak is a soldier, honored in Scripture for leading God's people into battle against larger and better-armed enemies. Judges 4 tells of God's people triumphing over their enemies under the leadership of Deborah and Barak through the historical viewpoint as we see it on the earth. Judges 5 retells the same story from the cosmic perspective of God sending the stars into battle, bringing the rain that flooded enemies, and delivering His people. Even though the men fought under the strategy of Deborah and the battlefield leadership of Barak, it was the Lord who brought the victory over His enemies as "the LORD routed Sisera and all his chariots and all his army before Barak by the edge of the sword…all the army of Sisera fell by the edge of the sword; not a man was left."[a]

The fact that a smaller army of lesser-skilled men was completely victorious is because of God. Judges 5:20-22 explains that God sent an incredible rain that flooded the path of the 900 iron chariots, bogging them down in the mud and making them easy targets for death: "From heaven the

---

[a] Judges 4:15-16

stars fought, from their courses they fought against Sisera. The torrent Kishon swept them away, the ancient torrent, the torrent Kishon. March on, my soul, with might! Then loud beat the horses' hoofs with the galloping, galloping of his steeds." Barak is like many men. He is a believer who trusts the Lord, but he struggles with courage and tends to be timid, making it difficult for him to step forward as a courageous leader. Thankfully, God is patient and gracious with Barak—a bit like a father helping encourage and mature a beloved son.

Dig Deeper.
1. To learn more about Barak, read Judges 4-5.

Walk it out. Talk it out.
1. What surprises you about the faith and failure of Barak? Why?
2. In what ways can you relate to Barak's combination of faith and fear?
3. How is a wise counselor like Deborah important to have in your life? Who do you look to for wise counsel?
4. How can group members be praying for each other this week?

HEBREWS 11

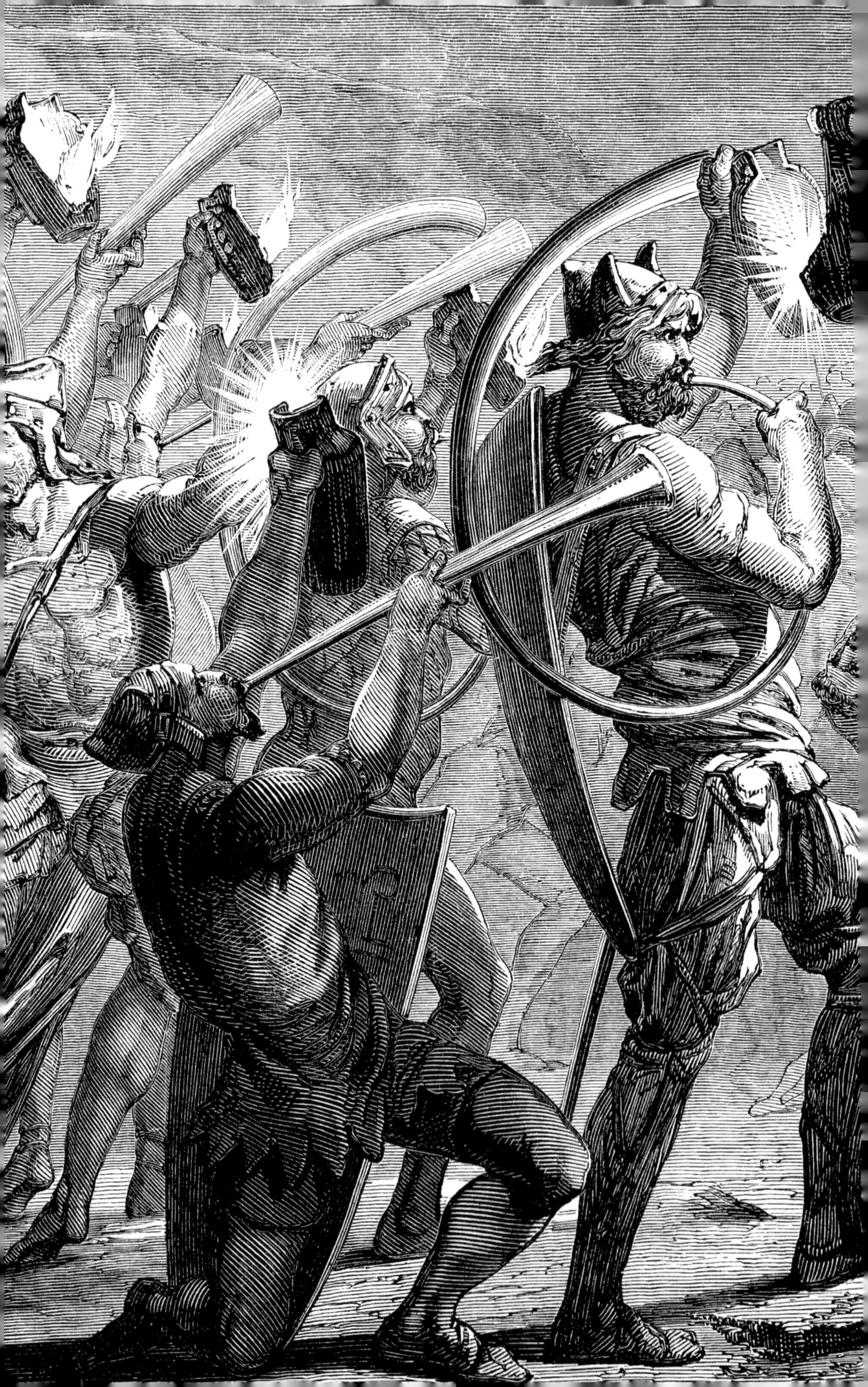

GIDEON

Chapter 13: Faith for Gideon
Hebrews 11:32

Hebrews 11:32 – And what more shall I say? For time would fail me to tell of Gideon, Barak, Samson, Jephthah…

Gideon's story in Judges 6-8 opens with both the Israelites and their enemy, the Midianites, doing "evil in the sight of the Lord." God's patience wears out with His people, and He allows Midian to undertake a successful terrorist invasion.

For the ensuing seven years, the Israelites—who are supposed to be God's people but live in open, constant, rebellious sin—are forced into hiding in the mountains while their enemies move into their homes, plunder their possessions, and eat their livestock and crops. Today, the news would report this as an invasion causing a humanitarian crisis rather than a consequence for grave sin.

Then, everything changes when "the people of Israel cried out for help to the LORD."[a] This is the Judges cycle—people do evil, God does not intervene to save them, their lives plunge into suffering and darkness, and eventually, under great pain and loss, as a last resort, they cry out to God. Sadly, many people do the same thing today—and only when they have hit proverbial rock bottom do they turn to God.

Jesus Christ then appears as "the angel [or messenger] of the Lord"[b] from Heaven. Jesus visits Gideon, who is hiding out and threshing wheat in a winepress. The scene is absolute poverty and cowardice. In a bit of comedic satire, Jesus calls Gideon, "O mighty man of valor."[c]

Gideon struggles with fear and anxiety, with his fear being mentioned seven different times.[d] Many people are just like him, struggling to move from fear to faith. Faith is not the absence of fear but instead the overcoming of fear. The most frequent command in the Bible in some form or fashion is "fear not," and often nearby God says in some manner the same thing that Jesus says to Gideon: "The LORD is with you[.]"[e]

---

[a] Judges 6:6 [b] Judges 6:11 [c] Judges 6:12 [d] Judges 6:15, 6:17, 6:22, 6:27, 6:37, 6:39, 7:11
[e] Judges 6:12

Gideon's fear rises when Jesus tells him His plan to send him to lead a counteroffensive, exchanging farming for fighting terrorist invaders. Gideon responds in fear, saying that his clan is the smallest and he's the runt in the litter. Nonetheless, Jesus promises the secret to success: "I will be with you, and you shall strike the Midianites[.]"[a] God promises victory will come, and Gideon struggles to believe it.

Gideon's Faith

However, Gideon also has some faith, as he asks Jesus for a sign and eventually obeys. Gideon is a lot like us—a mixture of faith and fear in trusting God's promises and commands. Even though Jesus says, "[Y]ou shall not die,"[b] Gideon struggles to fully trust the Lord in obedience. If we are honest, none of us has consistently responded to God's call on our lives to do difficult, if not seemingly impossible, things with pure faith that lacked any doubt or fear.

Then, Gideon got a big faith test:

> That night the LORD said to him, "Take your father's bull, and the second bull...and pull down the altar of Baal that your father has, and cut down the Asherah that is beside it and build an altar to the LORD your God on the top of the stronghold here...Then take the second bull and offer it as a burnt offering with the wood of the Asherah that you shall cut down." So Gideon took ten men of his servants and did as the LORD had told him. But because he was too afraid of his family and the men of the town to do it by day, he did it by night.[c]

Here we see Gideon's combination of faith as he obeyed God "that night," which indicates immediate obedience, and his fear in coming by night in hiding to tear down his father's altar. Despite his imperfections, Gideon is listed among the heroes of the faith in Hebrews 11 because he imperfectly trusted a perfect

---

[a] Judges 6:16 [b] Judges 6:23 [c] Judges 6:25-27

God.

The time then comes for Gideon, called and anointed by God the Holy Spirit, to lead a small group of untrained civilians against armed invading soldiers who had terrorized the nation for seven years. God knew that if the number of men with Gideon in the fight was too many, their pride would cause them to not see His sovereign hand giving them the victory and instead say, "My own hand has saved me."[a] Gideon's call to arms brought out 22,000 men. Anyone who was "fearful and trembling" was given the opportunity to not fight and go home. This is a reasonable civilian response to urban combat. At this invitation, 12,000 start the long walk home, with 10,000 soldiers remaining. God then narrows the soldiers down to only 300 men for the fight. God's plan for Gideon was to bring 300 untrained, malnourished civilians into a war against 135,000 armed terrorists![b]

God senses Gideon's fear, and, like a good Father, He leads him through it into the biggest risk of his entire life, with the lives of 300 other men hanging in the balance. To be sure, God had promised them victory. However, when the enemy has 450 bad guys for each one of your men, it is easy to understand a bit of fear.

Now filled with faith and the Spirit, Gideon followed God's battle plan. Attacking at night would have been unexpected and a strategic surprise element. Rather than fighting, Gideon trusts the Lord to defeat the massive army, and their job was to worship God in faith and cause the enemy to worry in fear. Instead of taking up swords, the men filled jars with torches and took trumpets to blow. Gideon instructed them, "When I blow the trumpet, I and all who are with me, then blow the trumpets also on every side of all the camp and shout, 'For the LORD and for Gideon.'"[c] The soldiers "blew the trumpets and smashed the jars,"[d] essentially simply standing still as an act of worship and watching God do all the defeating and saving. Judges 7:21 reports, "[T]he LORD set every man's sword against his comrade and against all the army." The surprise

[a] Judges 7:2 [b] Judges 8:4-12 [c] Judges 7:18 [d] Judges 7:19

late-night attack, with the great noise and show of fire, created an illusion, causing the enemy camp to think they were being overtaken by a massive show of force. Filled with fear, the enemy panicked, with men grabbing swords and attacking one another in the darkness of night, killing their own comrades.

This victory delivered God's people from seven years of terrorism and made Gideon a war hero. However, Gideon's final days are not as noble.

Gideon's Failure

In the closing scenes of Gideon's life[a], God is silent. Gideon is not acting out of obedience to the Lord; instead, he is acting on his own. To use the language of the New Testament, Gideon remains a believer but goes from living in the Spirit to living in the flesh.

Gideon wrongly berates and publicly humiliates the elders in a town. Gideon then returned to the town of Penuel, where "he broke down the tower of Penuel and killed the men of the city."[b] Gideon is now attacking cities in his own nation and killing its citizens, who are his countrymen.

In confronting the Midianite kings Zebah and Zalmunna, Gideon is being driven by bitterness. God had already proven fully capable of justice, taking down an entire enemy army while Gideon and his men worshiped. In this instance, however, Gideon will not leave things in God's hands but instead takes vengeance because the kings murdered his brothers. The Old Testament does give a provision for a close relative to exact revenge for murder[c]; however, it appears that Gideon's brothers died in a military battle with Midianite soldiers under the leadership of the two kings, which would not qualify as justifiable execution. In a dark twist, Gideon then orders his firstborn son, Jether, to "[r]ise and kill them!"[d] Fearful, the boy does not kill the kings, which may have been a good thing, because it could have put a bounty on his head for the rest of his life. God says that vengeance is His and has proven this

---

[a] Judges 8 [b] Judges 8:17 [c] Leviticus 24:17, Deuteronomy 19:21 cf. Numbers 35:6-34 [d] Judges 8:20

fact by routing the enemy armies, but on this day, vengeance is Gideon's, as "Gideon arose and killed Zebah and Zalmunna[.]"ᵃ

Making matters worse, Gideon then "took the crescent ornaments that were on the necks of their camels."ᵇ Looking much like the modern-day crescent moon that serves as the symbol for Islam, this pagan jewelry with clear demonic association is moon-shaped, either of gold or silver, and worn by the Midianite kings or their camels. In Isaiah 3:18, God promises to judge these demonic pagan symbols as "…the Lord will take away…the crescents…"⁴⁹

Seeking to make Gideon into a king with a generational monarchy,

> the men of Israel said to Gideon, "Rule over us, you and your son and your grandson also, for you have saved us from the hand of Midian." Gideon said to them, "I will not rule over you, and my son will not rule over you; the LORD will rule over you."

In rejecting this offer to rule, Gideon is acting in faith and obedience. Rightly, Gideon declines the offer, and later God would raise up David to be their Spirit-filled warrior king instead.

However, Gideon then operates in unbelief and disobedience, saying, "[E]very one of you give me the earrings from his spoil." (For they had golden earrings…)"ᶜ A Bible commentary says, "The total collected equal just over forty pounds of gold! To this are added a variety of other items taken from the two kings and their camels. But such a significant amount represents only the beginning of all that has been gathered from the devastated Midianites."⁵⁰

Exodus 32:1-4 reports a very dark moment in the days of Moses when the people chose to worship a golden calf, which is the ancient symbol of the demon god Baal. As a younger man, Gideon destroyed an altar to Baal in his hometown of Ophrah, and he worships God. Now, he builds an altar to Baal in that

---

ᵃ Judges 8:21 ᵇ Judges 8:21 ᶜ Judges 8:24

same town. Tragically, he is following the unfaithful example of his father and reverting back to generational sin patterns. The final scenes of Gideon's life are that God's battle victory through him brought 40 years of peace. He took many wives, fathered 70 sons, lived to a "good old age," and "was buried in the tomb of Joash his father."[a]

Despite sexual sin and polygamy, the final lines of Gideon's life are haunting, showing that despite his imperfections, Gideon was godlier than the rest of the nation.

> As soon as Gideon died, the people of Israel turned again and whored after the Baals and made Baal-berith their god. And the people of Israel did not remember the LORD their God, who had delivered them from the hand of all their enemies on every side, and they did not show steadfast love to the family of Jerubbaal (that is, Gideon) in return for all the good that he had done to Israel.[b]

In Judges, the focus then shifts to Gideon's son Abimelech, whose name means "my father is king." Abimelech was raised apart from his father, which likely caused a father wound after being born to a non-Israelite "concubine"—an ancient combination of adulterer, lover, nanny, and prostitute. In Judges 9, Abimelech deceives and murders all but one of Gideon's other sons and publicly campaigns to be king once those men in line in front of him are dead by his hand. Abimelech rules as an illegitimate king for three years, in complete defiance against God who said the time for a king had not yet come. God opposes and ultimately destroys Abimelech, who worships demons and seeks to rule Israel like Satan sought to rule Heaven.[c] In shame, Abimelech finds his end when a woman drops a millstone on his head, crushing his skull, and he asks his armor-bearer to run him through with a sword so that he would not have been killed by a woman.

In Judges, especially the final scenes of Gideon's life, we see

[a] Judges 8:28-32 [b] Judges 8:33-35 [c] Revelation 12:7-11

that God is perfect, and His leaders are not. Their success is by His grace, not their goodness. That should encourage us that, for God to use us, we don't need to be perfect. However, our sins can cause incredible pain and loss for generations. Lastly, it is not too far-fetched to assume that Gideon did indeed repent of his sins against the Lord. After all, some of them were private matters that we would not know about unless he told his testimony and included mention of the sins he committed but God forgave.

Our Faithful God

Faith is like a muscle; it gets stronger the more we use it.
Throughout the Gideon story, we see God repeatedly show up in supernatural ways. Not only did the Holy Spirit clothe Gideon, but Jesus also came down from Heaven to speak with him, God later spoke to him again, and God gave him a prophetic dream with a correct interpretation. These miraculous moments reveal the freedom and power of God as He works differently in the lives of different people and leaders. Seeing that God is truly with him, Gideon grows in his faith. Judges 7:15 reports, "As soon as Gideon heard the telling of the dream and its interpretation, he worshiped." God keeps showing up and speaking to Gideon to mature his faith and compel him to action. Without these moments, Gideon would have never been a triumphant warrior.

Although Gideon is honored as a man of faith in Hebrews 11, his work is imperfect, and the change he brings is temporary. This sets the stage for the coming of Jesus Christ, whose Father truly is King. Born of a virgin instead of a concubine, Jesus grows up to live without sin and is the greater Gideon. Continually humble, Jesus will return to the nation of Israel to establish Himself as King forever and Judge over all nations. On that day, a trumpet blast like the days of Gideon will announce His riding into battle with an angelic army mightier than Gideon's. Jesus Christ will perfectly execute justice against His enemies and deliver God's people to worship Him alone forever without ever reverting to idolatry.

Furthermore, on that day, the ultimate King, Warrior, and Judge—Jesus Christ—will sentence all demons, including Baal and Asherah, "into the eternal fire prepared for the devil and his angels."[a]

Dig Deeper.

1. To learn more about Gideon, read Judges 6-8.

Walk it out. Talk it out.

1. What most surprises you about the faith and failure of Gideon? Why?
2. Are there any ways that you relate to Gideon?
3. How does the story of Gideon show us that the sins we commit can impact generations of our family legacy? What is God's message to you personally in his tragic example?
4. How can group members be praying for each other this week?

---

[a] Matthew 25:41

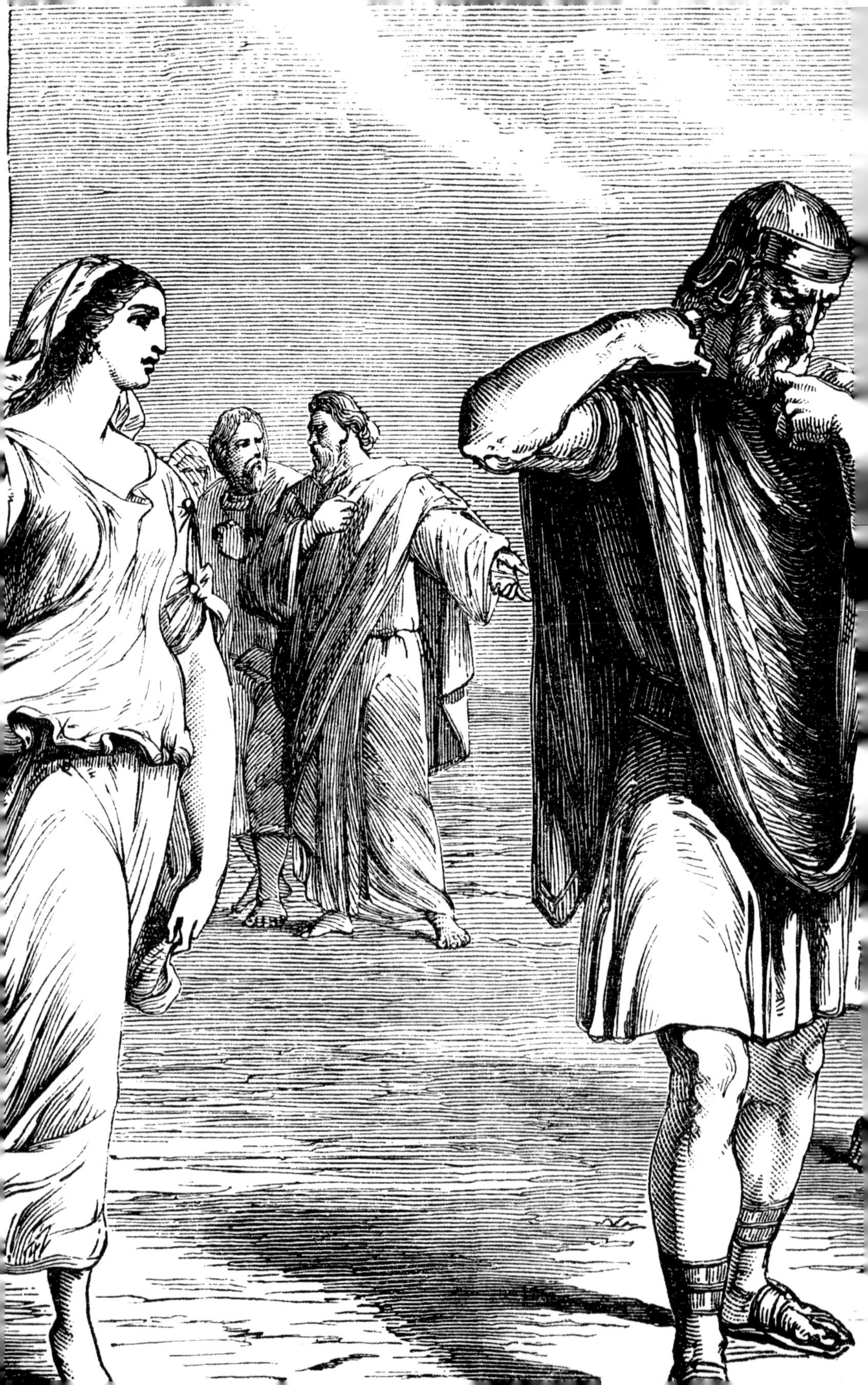

JEPHTHAH

Chapter 14: Faith for Jephthah
Hebrews 11:32

Hebrews 11:32 – And what more shall I say? For time would fail me to tell of Gideon, Barak, Samson, Jephthah...

The story of Jephthah is found in one chapter of the Bible—Judges 11—and his story is a tragic one: "[H]e was the son of a prostitute."[a] His father, Gilead, also had other sons with his wife. This caused Jephthah to be hated and rejected:

> ...when his wife's sons grew up, they drove Jephthah out saying, "You shall not have an inheritance in our father's house, for you are the son of another woman." Then Jephthah fled from his brothers and lived in the land of Tob, and worthless fellows collected around Jephthah and went out with him.

A hard life made Jephthah into a hard man. Tough as nails, fighting for his life, having been cast out and disowned by his own father and family, he became "a mighty warrior."[b] He becomes a bandit leader—an outlaw living on the run. Some time later, "the Ammonites made war against Israel."[c] Needing a wartime general to save the people in peril, his family and hometown of Gilead sought out Jephthah and pledged that if he would lead them in war, he could be "head and leader over them."[d]

Jephthah's Faith

Jephthah sought to negotiate a peace agreement, to no avail. He proves himself to be a strong, wise, and competent leader—heads and shoulders above his brothers and other men in that day.

He eventually leads God's people to a total victory, as they captured both the land and their enemies. The backdrop for

[a] Judges 11:1 [b] Judges 11:1 [c] Judges 11:4 [d] Judges 11:11

this war was spiritual warfare against "Chemosh your god."[a] Chemosh was a demonic false god, often mentioned in the Old Testament as a chief enemy against the Lord. The worship of Chemosh included child sacrifice, as well as adult sacrifice, and a Bible dictionary reports the fact that "upon occasion he might be worshiped with human sacrifices is probable from 2 K[ings] 3:27, where the king of Moab offered his eldest son as a burnt-offering."[51] Chemosh literally means "conqueror," as he was a fierce military demon. Therefore, Jephthah's conquest of his army revealed the greatness of the One True God.

Following his great victory, Jephthah appears as a preacher, proclaiming the greatness of his God to the conquered king: "'I therefore have not sinned against you, and you do me wrong by making war on me. The Lord, the Judge, decide this day between the people of Israel and the people of Ammon.' But the king of the Ammonites did not listen to the words of Jephthah that he sent to him."[b]

The story of Jephthah's life until this point is incredible. The son of a prostitute rejected by his family and hometown grows up to love and serve the Lord as a military war hero. Tragically, the story does not end there.

Jephthah's Failure

We will now study Jephthah's rash vow. This scene is one of the most shocking and devastating in all of Scripture. The story starts,

> And Jephthah made a vow to the Lord and said, "If you will give the Ammonites into my hand, then whatever comes out from the doors of my house to meet me when I return in peace from the Ammonites shall be the Lord's, and I will offer it up for a burnt offering."[c]

After triumphing in battle, Jephthah returned home, and the story continues.

---

[a] Judges 11:24 [b] Judges 11:27-28 [c] Judges 11:30-31

And behold, his daughter came out to meet him with tambourines and with dances. She was his only child; besides her he had neither son nor daughter. And as soon as he saw her, he tore his clothes and said, "Alas, my daughter! You have brought me very low, and you have become the cause of great trouble to me. For I have opened my mouth to the Lord, and I cannot take back my vow." And she said to him, "My father, you have opened your mouth to the Lord; do to me according to what has gone out of your mouth, now that the Lord has avenged you on your enemies, on the Ammonites." So she said to her father, "Let this thing be done for me: leave me alone two months, that I may go up and down on the mountains and weep for my virginity, I and my companions." So he said, "Go." Then he sent her away for two months, and she departed, she and her companions, and wept for her virginity on the mountains. And at the end of two months, she returned to her father, who did with her according to his vow that he had made. She had never known a man, and it became a custom in Israel that the daughters of Israel went year by year to lament the daughter of Jephthah the Gileadite four days in the year.[a]

As a father, I cannot read those haunting lines without feeling sick to my stomach and fighting back tears. In a moment of rash foolishness, Jephthah made a vow to the Lord that would destroy his family and only child—a beloved daughter who adored and celebrated her father. In the story, the young woman demonstrates incredible faith—giving her own life to fulfill her father's rash, tragic vow. Her faith is indeed greater than her father's. Her story was so tragic that a national holiday was celebrated every year by the young women in tribute to her life and death.

Christians have understandably struggled to make sense of this story. The Bible repeatedly forbids human sacrifice, the very thing that the demon god Chemosh required of his

[a] Judges 11:34-40

worshipers before being defeated by Jephthah and his God. Bible commentators have speculated in numerous ways about how to interpret this scene. A Bible Dictionary provides some helpful interpretive clues:

> ...readers should know Jephthah's vow—an attempt to ensure God's assistance—is entirely unnecessary...[it] however, points to Jephthah's sorrowful declaration as an indication that he did not intend her to be the sacrifice... In the account, God neither authorizes nor approves of the vow and its fulfillment...Jephthah makes and executes the vow of his own volition and must reap the consequences of his folly...The message to the reader is not about God's take on the sacrifice, but Jephthah's failure and lack of faith.[52]

It is perplexing that Jephthah is included in Hebrews 11, the chapter most known in the Bible regarding faith. The people in his day were completely godless, and though, in comparison, he is a godly man, he has one tragic day when he makes one faithless and frightful vow to God. He did not need to make that vow. God was going to give the victory, and he apparently waned in faith and sought to strengthen his position with God entering battle by making a rash, horrific vow. As a leader of the people with a high public profile and responsibility to set an example, his sinful choice serves, to this day, as a sobering and terrifying reminder that even godly people can undo their greatest blessings with a moment of faithlessness.

Our Faithful God

The story of Jephthah reveals that his failures are his fault, and his successes are God's grace. Before heading into battle, he told the leaders of Gilead, "[I]f... the Lord gives them over to me..."[a] He is fully aware that victory in battle was only possible

---

[a] Judges 11:9

by God's divine intervention and, in advance, he gives God the glory and credit for the eventual military victory.

It is indeed God who gives them victory: "…the Lord, the God of Israel, gave Sihon and all his people into the hand of Israel, and they defeated them."[a] Over and over, it is God who is the hero of every story in the Bible. It is God who defeats enemies and delivers His people.

Much like the other judges who served the Lord, the secret to Jephthah's success was the Spirit of God. He had a unique anointing that empowered him to lead God's people into triumph over their fierce enemies: "Then the Spirit of the LORD was upon Jephthah…"[b] God worked in and through Jephthah and the other judges.

The judges underscore the paradox that runs through the whole of Hebrews 11: God's perfect work gets done through imperfect people. In each case, divine victory emerges not from human strength but through weakness. The Lord is the true Judge and Deliverer[c], and it is He who orchestrates salvation in ways that confound human logic. Gideon's victory comes through weakness, Barak's through dependency, Jephthah's through zealously misdirected loyalty, and Samson's through sacrificial death, which we will study next.

Hebrews presents these figures not as heroes to emulate in every detail but as witnesses to the God who works through flawed faith to accomplish His purposes. A Bible commentator says, "This is the Judge who stands behind the judges."[53]

God's decision to work through such morally complicated figures reaffirms the New Testament's teaching that His strength is made perfect in weakness.[d] Each judge anticipates the greater Deliverer to come. Like Barak, Jesus entrusted Himself to the Father's voice; like Gideon, Christ conquered not through armies but through weakness; like Jephthah, He was rejected by His own; and like Samson, He triumphed through death. Yet unlike them, He is without sin. Their lives serve as foils that heighten the glory of Christ, the true and faithful Judge and Deliverer of God's people. We will learn about Samson next,

[a] Judges 11:21 [b] Judges 11:29 [c] Judges 11:27 [d] 2 Corinthians 12:9

since he is the final judge in the book of Judges.

Dig Deeper.

1. To learn more about Jephthah, read Judges 11.

Walk it out. Talk it out.

1. What most surprises you about the faith and failure of Jephthah?
2. How surprised are you to see Jephthah listed in Hebrews 11 as a man of faith in light of the rash vow regarding his daughter?
3. What personal lesson did the Holy Spirit impress upon you as you studied the life of Jephthah?
4. How can group members be praying for one another this week?

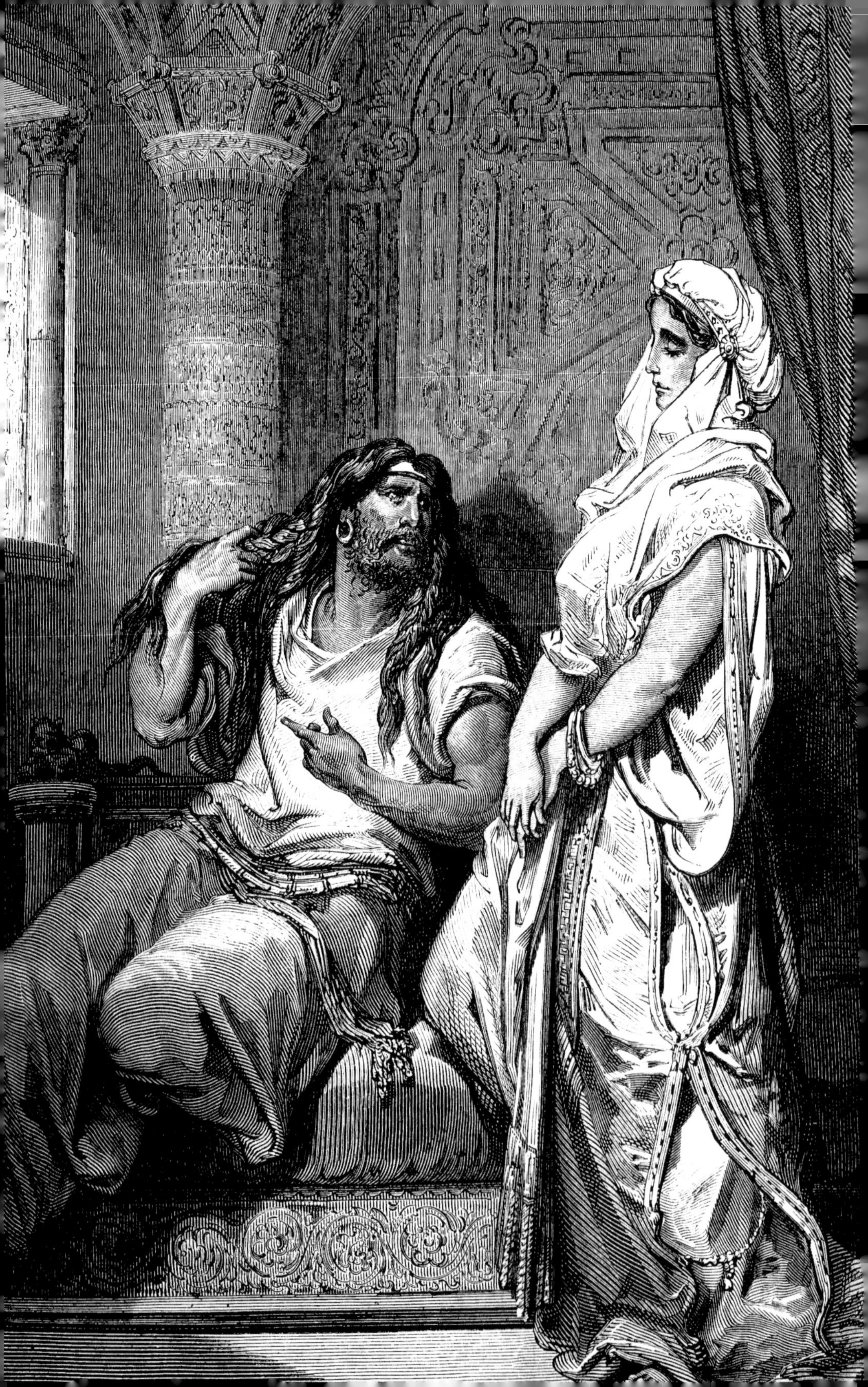

SAMSON

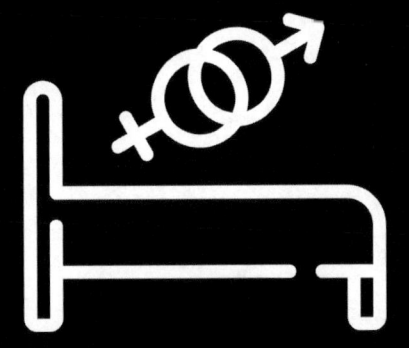

Chapter 15: Faith for Samson
Hebrews 11:32

Hebrews 11:32 – And what more shall I say? For time would fail me to tell of Gideon, Barak, Samson, Jephthah...

In life, many people learn from their mistakes, make moral progress as they age, and eventually start passing their tests in the school of hard knocks. However, on occasion, we meet someone whose life is a befuddling, head-scratching series of decades spent doing the same stupid thing over and over until their life implodes and ends.

Samson is one of those guys. His name means "sunny," but, sadly, he is not very bright. God cared for him, but he did not care much for God. God pursued him, but he did not pursue God. God blessed him, but he did not bless God. God told him what not to do, and that is precisely what he did.
Samson is the last of the 12 judges, and his history is reported in Judges 13-16. The 96 verses about him are more than any other person in Judges. The only other place Samson is mentioned in the Bible is Hebrews 11.

Samson was raised up as a judge by God during a brutal time when God's people were ruled by their enemies, the Philistines. This period of foreign rule over Israel—20 years—was the longest of any of the judges. Unlike previous oppression, the people never called out to the Lord. Despite being ruled by terrorists and tormented by demons, there was no interest in God. The nation had hit a truly low point, and God raised up Samson to spend his adult life as a one-man wrecking ball at war with the Philistines.

Samson's parents seemed to be godly, though his unnamed, barren mother appeared more spiritually mature than his father, Manoah. They both wanted a child, and an angel, or "messenger," of the Lord (likely Jesus Christ) appeared twice in Judges 13, telling the couple a son would be born and that he needed to live under a Nazirite vow in service to the Lord as a warrior against the Philistines. (Numbers 6:1-21 gives the terms of the vow—restriction from alcohol, avoidance of unclean foods, no haircuts, and not touching unclean, dead corpses.) Eventually, Samson violates every single one of these vows.

In Judges 14, Samson appears as a typical meathead who bosses his parents around, demanding they find a Philistine young woman to marry him. This is clearly sinful, as these were the enemies of God and His people.[a] God would bend this wrong for right, as the marriage gave Samson closer access to the Philistines so he could war against them. Judges 14:4 says, "His father and mother did not know that it was from the LORD, for he was seeking an opportunity against the Philistines. At that time, the Philistines ruled over Israel."

The fact that God can save and use someone as flawed as Samson should encourage us; even when we have done wrong, God can and will do right and even use our bad for His good. God is very gracious. In Samson's life, and our own, God does not command or condone sin, but He does control the outcome because He is sovereign and good. Samson is empowered by the Holy "Spirit of the Lord" with powers a bit like modern-day comic superheroes.

Sadly, Samson attends a pagan party with the young Philistine men, replete with excessive drinking and sexual sin of every kind. Samson poses a riddle to 30 men as part of gambling, and the men threatened to kill his wife and burn down her father's home if she did not divulge the answer to the riddle. She coaxes Samson for the answer, so he murders the 30 men and moves back in with his parents, abandoning his wife, who is later remarried.

Samson's Faith

In Judges 15, the Holy Spirit empowered Samson to escape arrest and slaughter 1000 enemies with nothing more than the jawbone of a donkey that happened to be lying nearby. Scenes like this in Samson's life are surreal—one man without a weapon or a battle plan killing 1000 men who are fighting him at the same time. Samson tried to get his wife back only to

[a] Deuteronomy 7:3-4

FLAWED BUT FAITHFUL

find that her father remarried her to a Philistine man because she had been abandoned. Angry, Samson somehow found the time to catch 300 foxes, which is not an easy task, tie their tails together, set them on fire, and send them racing to the stacks of grain and orchards, destroying the Philistines' food supply and livelihood. The Philistines responded by burning his ex-wife and her father to death. In pure vengeance, as their war is escalating, "Samson said…'I swear I will be avenged on you, and after that I will quit.' And he struck them hip and thigh with a great blow…"[a]

A bit like a Hebrew Rambo, the one-man wrecking crew then went camping in the cleft of a rock while his enemies formed an angry mob to kill him. Joining them were 3000 Hebrews, as his own people turned against him and sided with the Philistines! To both sides of the conflict, Samson was considered a terrorist; the one thing to which these enemies could agree was that the biggest threat to them was the Spirit-filled son of Manoah. Samson willingly allowed the Hebrews to take him as a prisoner of war and bound him with many ropes. Judges 15:14-17 describes the scene as they handed him over to the Philistines:

> [T]he Spirit of the LORD rushed upon him, and the ropes that were on his arms became as flax that has caught fire, and his bonds melted off his hands. And he found a fresh jawbone of a donkey, and put out his hand and took it, and with it he struck 1,000 men. And Samson said, "With the jawbone of a donkey, heaps upon heaps, with the jawbone of a donkey have I struck down a thousand men." As soon as he had finished speaking, he threw away the jawbone out of his hand. And that place was called Ramath-lehi [meaning Jawbone Hill].

The entire Samson story is one of escalating violence caused by vengeful revenge. Samson says this very fact in Judges 15:11:

---

[a] Judges 15:7-8

"As they did to me, so have I done to them."

Samson is driven by anger and motivated by pleasure. When he finally does pray, it's a selfish prayer that sounds more like scolding God for not getting him a drink. Samson treats his God a bit like a bad waitress who has failed to fill up his glass. God, very kindly, does not strike him dead but instead brings forth water from a rock, which sounds a lot like the days of Moses.

The final chapter of his life starts in Judges 16:1, saying, "Samson went to Gaza, and there he saw a prostitute, and he went in to her." Samson's arrogance is on full display. Alone and unarmed, he walks into enemy territory to spend time at a brothel, fearing no one and nothing. Oddly, he is likely the only believer in town and perhaps the worst missionary in the history of the world.

Unable to be defeated by armies of men, Samson is about to be chopped down by one woman. Judges 16:4 says, "After this he loved a woman in the Valley of Sorek, whose name was Delilah." Curiously, this woman lives down in a valley, closer to Hell, and the man with a strong body and weak mind is carelessly wandering into disaster.

The capture of Samson was regarded by his enemies as their demon god defeating his God. For them, the entire conflict was spiritual warfare. A Bible dictionary says:

> The Canaanites were already worshiping Dagon, a grain god, when the Philistines arrived. The Philistines assimilated him into their pantheon, and over time he became their chief god. They built temples to him in Ashdod (1 Sam 5:1–2), Gaza (Judges 16:21–23), and possibly Beth Shan, as well (1 Chronicles 10:10; 1 Samuel 31:10). After Saul was killed in battle, the Philistines "put his armor in the temple of their gods and fastened his head in the temple of Dagon" (1 Chronicles 10:10).[54]

In his final days, Samson got duped by a likely Philistine prostitute named Delilah. The Philistine lords paid her 1,100 pieces of silver in exchange for learning the secret to Samson's strength. Lying to her repeatedly, Samson avoided being taken captive. Finally, the weak-willed man told the Black Widow double agent that if they cut his hair, he would lose his strength. While Samson slept on Delilah's lap, his head was shaved, and he lost his strength because "the Lord had left him."[a] A Bible Dictionary says,

> The Philistines put out his eyes, took him to Gaza, bound him, and made him a grinder in the prison (Judges 16:21). However, Samson's hair began to grow back (Judges 16:22). While the Philistine lords celebrated their capture of Samson with a festival devoted to their god Dagon, they summoned Samson to come and perform for them (Judges 16:23–24). When Samson was situated between the pillars of their temple, he asked his guide to put his hands on the temple pillars (Judges 16:25–26). The Lord granted Samson strength one last time, and Samson was able to push the pillars of the temple down, killing all the Philistines who were in it (Judges 16:29–30). Samson killed more Philistines with his death than he had with his life (Judges 16:30). His brothers and the rest of his father's house then took his body and buried him between Zorah and Eshtaol, in his father's burial place (Judges 16:31).[55]

Samson's suicidal death was also a significant military defeat of his enemies. A Bible dictionary says:

> During the times of the judges and kings of Israel, the Philistines were largely under the leadership of the five lords...of the Philistine pentapolis: Gaza, Ashdod, Ashkelon, Gath, and Ekron. These rulers both collaborated (1 Sam 5:8) and disputed with one another (1 Sam 29:1–11)—none of them exercised authority over all the Philistines. When Samson destroyed the temple to Dagon, all five were killed[.] (Judges 16:27, 30)[56]

[a] Judges 16:20

Samson's Failure

Although one of the most famous people in the Bible, Samson's life is rarely taught because it is so complex. As a Bible dictionary says, "No biblical character is more paradoxical than Samson (Judges 13–16). A figure of heroic physical strength, he is also a morally and emotionally weak person whose frailty is highlighted by the tragic pattern of the OT story."[57]

When things are going poorly, it's common to hear phrases like "things went downhill fast" or there was a "downward spiral." The scenes of Samson's life are introduced by saying he "went down."

- Judges 14:1: Samson went down to Timnah, and at Timnah he saw one of the daughters of the Philistines.
- Judges 14:5: …Samson went down with his father and mother to Timnah…
- Judges 14:7: [H]e went down and talked with the woman, and she was right in Samson's eyes.
- Judges 14:10: His father went down to the woman, and Samson prepared a feast there, for so the young men used to do.
- Judges 14:19: [H]e went down to Ashkelon and struck down thirty men of the town and took their spoil…

Samson repeatedly "went down"—physically, spiritually, and morally. He crosses all boundaries and has no regard for what is right. He repeatedly is with people and in places he, as a believer, should not be, especially as one who is supposed to be leading others as a judge. His example is negative, and in this way, Samson looks a lot like everyone else in his day.

Our Faithful God

In Judges 13, it is likely Jesus Christ who appears twice to Samson's parents, telling them he would be born as a warrior for God. Judges 13:22 says, "And Manoah said to his wife, 'We shall surely die, for we have seen God.'"

By all accounts, Samson went to Heaven, but because of his sinful rejection of God's anointing and constantly living in the flesh instead of the Spirit, his life was Hell on earth. He was constantly in fights, seeking love and never finding it, known to carouse with prostitutes, never had one friend, and died by suicide as a blind captive in war, having been betrayed by his wife as a lonely, broken man with no children to even pray for him. Sometimes, the difference in behavior between a believer and an unbeliever is a blurry line. One thing is for sure: like Samson, if we live in the flesh, life will feel like Hell even if we die and go to Heaven.

For Christians, the question of how Samson could be so anointed by the Holy Spirit and yet so ungodly is a mystery. Sadly, he does not make moral progress throughout his life; he is a carnal and sinful man whom God apparently loved and saved by pure grace. The work of the Holy Spirit in the life of Samson is truly incredible. Samson is divinely conceived, divinely dedicated, divinely destined, divinely empowered, and divinely blessed.

Throughout the story of Samson's life, the anointing of the Holy Spirit in power is said to enable the man to have superhuman strength to break free of strong bonds, kill a lion with his bare hands, and slaughter dozens and thousands of men, causing everyone, even his own countrymen, to fear him.

- Judges 13:25: [T]he Spirit of the Lord began to stir [Samson]…
- Judges 14:6: Then the Spirit of the Lord rushed upon him…
- Judges 14:19: [T]he Spirit of the Lord rushed upon him…
- Judges 15:14: [T]he Spirit of the Lord rushed upon him…

Sadly, Samson was so insensitive to the presence and power of the Holy Spirit in his life that, near its end, he didn't know the Holy Spirit had left him. Judges 16:20 reports, "'The Philistines are upon you, Samson!' And he awoke from his sleep and said, 'I will go out as at other times and shake myself free.' But he did not know that the Lord had left him."

Samson's life is a painful study in the difference between being saved by the Spirit, empowered by the Spirit, and having good character as the fruit of the Spirit. God saved and empowered Samson by grace, but he did not yield to the Holy Spirit—repenting of his sin and growing in godliness—to become an increasingly better man. Nonetheless, in comparison to the ungodly men in his day, his faith is greater than theirs, which just goes to show how utterly depraved that entire generation was.

Dig Deeper.
1. To learn more about Samson, read Judges 13-16.

Walk it out. Talk it out.
1. What most surprises you about the faith and failure of Samson?
2. Discuss as a group how ungodly even the "believers" had to be in Samson's day for him to be used of God.
3. What is the big lesson the Holy Spirit had for you to apply in your own life in the study of these four judges?
4. How can group members be praying for each other this week?

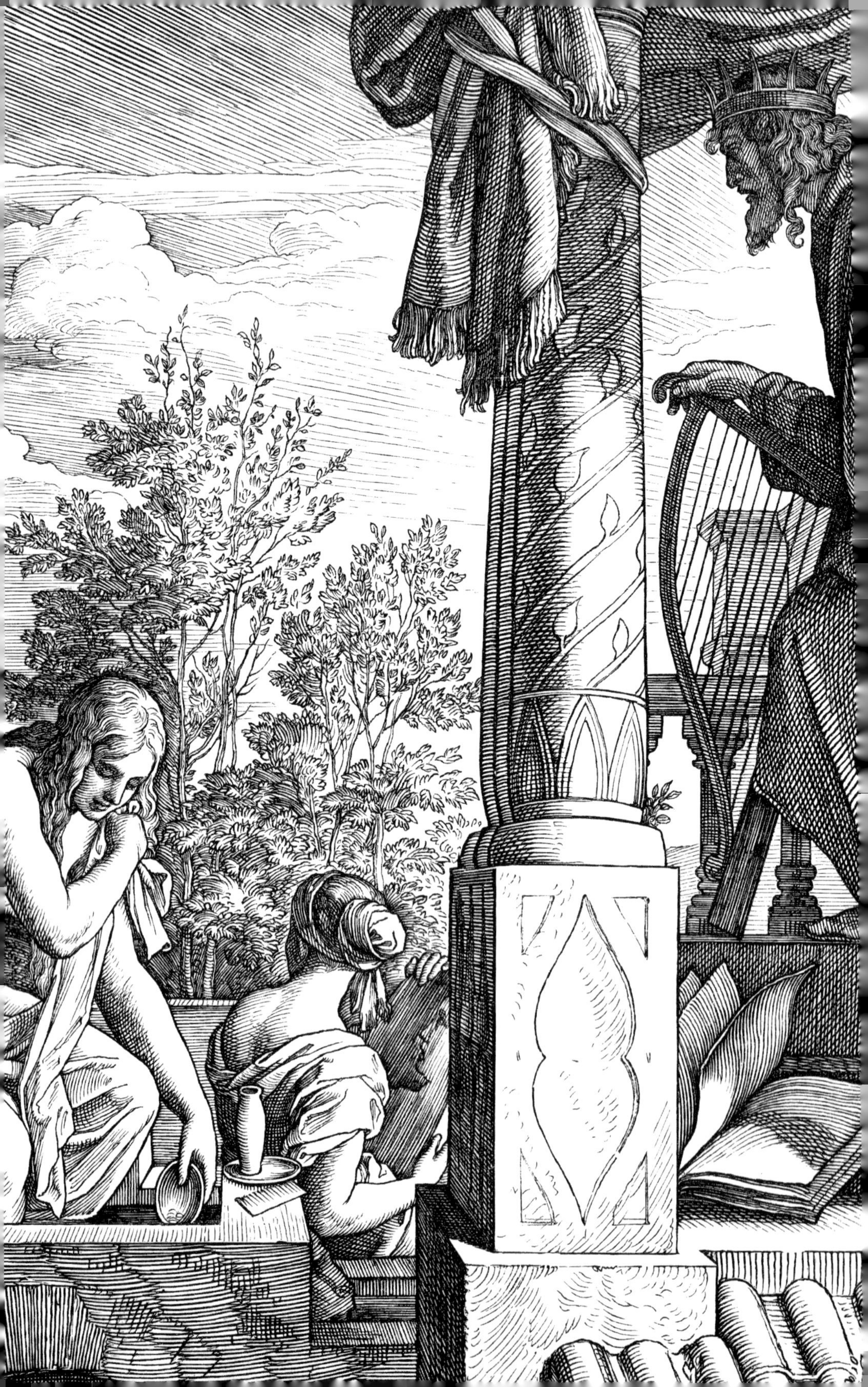

DAVID

Chapter 16: Faith for David
Hebrews 11:32

Hebrews 11:32 – And what more shall I say? For time would fail me to tell of...David...

Throughout human history, there are a few people who cast such a giant shadow that it would be difficult to imagine how different everything would be if they had never been born. This is precisely the case with David, whose name is mentioned over 1000 times in the Bible.

The Bible extensively discusses David, dedicating approximately 11% of its content to him across 126 chapters.[58] A Bible dictionary says, "David's story is really long. *Really* long. It is in fact the longest story about an individual in the Old Testament, and David is mentioned more in the OT [Old Testament] than any other human."[59]

David's Faith

David's story is prominently featured in 2 Samuel, which covers his 40-year reign over the united tribes of Israel, and 1 Chronicles, which focuses on his preparations for building God's temple. David is also credited with writing half of the Psalms in the Bible, with 73 directly attributed to him.

A Bible Dictionary says,

> Israel's second and greatest king, David rose to power from humble circumstances and amid many difficulties; he captured Jerusalem, established it as his capital, unified the nation, and built an empire that stretched from Egypt to Mesopotamia during a 40-year reign, ca. 1010–970 b.c.e. He was a man of many talents—a shepherd, musician, poet, warrior, politician, administrator—but he is most prominent as the king par excellence, as the standard for all later kings, and as a messianic symbol.[60]

David was known as "a man after [God's] own heart,"[a] who subdued enemies, unified the tribes, and ruled with justice, even penning songs that would nourish Israel's faith for generations.[b] David's faith is perhaps best known when, as a young man with a slingshot, he took down the mighty Philistine giant, Goliath.[c] However, he was also a sinner like the rest of us, as we will learn next.

David's Failure

David is a very passionate man. On his best days, that passion drove him to serve God with incredible faith. On his worst days, that passion drove him to sin against God with incredible failure. A Bible Dictionary says, "The Bible portrays David as a complex figure, both a champion chosen by God and a deeply flawed individual."[61]

The Bible does not shy away from depicting David's sins, such as his affair with Bathsheba and the subsequent orchestration of the murder of her husband, Uriah the Hittite.[d] The entire scene is quite awful. David, the mighty king, was atop his roof surveying his kingdom when he saw a "very beautiful" woman "bathing." His servants told him she was the married "wife of Uriah the Hittite." Committing adultery, "he lay with her," and she later told David, "I am pregnant."[e]

Rather than first repenting of his sin, David sought to cover it. Her husband, the devoted soldier Uriah the Hittite, was brought home from war by David with the intent of getting Uriah to sleep with his wife so that he would wrongly think that his wife's baby was his own and not David's! Uriah would not go home and sleep with his wife because he wanted to avoid enjoying something his fellow soldiers, who were deployed, were denied. This man had such integrity that he would not even enjoy his wife at the king's request. The next night, "David invited him, and he ate in his presence and drank, so that he made him drunk. And in the evening he went out to lie on his couch with the servants of his lord, but he did not go down to

---

[a] 1 Samuel 13:14; Acts 13:22 [b] 2 Sam. 8:1–15; Ps. 89 [c] 1 Samuel 17 [d] 2 Samuel 11-12
[e] 2 Samuel 11:2-5

his house."[a]

    Rather than taking the opportunity to repent, David sent Uriah back to battle. "In the morning David wrote a letter to Joab and sent it by the hand of Uriah. In the letter he wrote, 'Set Uriah in the forefront of the hardest fighting, and then draw back from him, that he may be struck down, and die.'"[b] The integrous Uriah did not even open the sealed letter that planned his murder, and he was killed in battle by David, who made it look like a normal loss in war. This was a murder and cover-up of the king's adultery and impregnating the wife of his faithful soldier. "When the wife of Uriah heard that Uriah her husband was dead, she lamented over her husband. And when the mourning was over, David sent and brought her to his house, and she became his wife and bore him a son. But the thing that David had done displeased the Lord."[c] Then, the prophet Nathan rebuked David to his face, the child died, and David and Bathsheba later birthed Solomon, a man who would later cause great grief by being a sexually immoral king like his father. A Bible dictionary says, "David had eight wives who are named in Scripture, seven of whom bore him children, the other being Michal, Saul's daughter (2 Sam 6:23); the most prominent were Abigail (1 Samuel 25) and Bathsheba (2 Samuel 11–12). He also had many unnamed wives and concubines, who likewise bore him children (1 Chr 3:9; 14:3)."[62]

    David's failures in fathering many children with many women also caused him to fail as a father and led to a lot of turmoil in the future generations of his family. In 2 Samuel 13-19, two of David's oldest sons are killed. The scenes leading up to God taking the lives of these sons are horrifying. First, David's oldest son, Amnon, raped his half-sister, Tamar. In vengeance, David's third son, Absalom, killed his brother and fled for his life. David is presented as a passive father not leading his family—grieving the awful character of his sons but not fathering them to godliness. David eventually brought Absalom back from exile, reconciling after the son kept begging to be restored to his father, but initially banished him for two

---

[a] 2 Samuel 11:13 [b] 2 Samuel 11:15-16 [c] 2 Samuel 11:26-27

years. Shortly thereafter, however, Absalom began organizing a subversive coup attempt against his father. King David was forced to flee from Jerusalem, along with his household and loyal soldiers. Absalom had a deep father wound and intense seething bitterness against his father, David. He appointed himself as king, dethroning his father, and took his father's concubines as his lovers to sleep with the same women! David eventually kills his son in battle and retakes his throne. In hearing of his son's death, despite the treasonous betrayal of his father,

> the king was deeply moved and went up to the chamber over the gate and wept. And as he went, he said, "O my son Absalom, my son, my son Absalom! Would I had died instead of you, O Absalom, my son, my son!"…So the victory that day was turned into mourning for all the people, for the people heard that day, "The king is grieving for his son."…The king covered his face, and the king cried with a loud voice, "O my son Absalom, O Absalom, my son, my son!"[a]

As if this story of David's failure as a father due to innumerable sexual sins was not enough, things get worse. David's decline and eventual death was fraught with a battle for succession to the throne between his oldest surviving son, Adonijah, and Bathsheba's favorite son, Solomon.[b] With David elderly and feeble, Adonijah sought to steal the throne, naming himself king. Under the manipulation of Bathsheba and the prophet Nathan, David decreed Solomon to be his successor, which led to more conflict within the various lines of David's descendants. On his deathbed, David asked that a list of men who wronged him be punished[c] by death with the shedding of their "blood."

Despite being a man guilty of some heinous sin, David is still called in Scripture by God "a man after my heart, who will do all my will."[d] The key to God's faithfulness to David is

[a] 2 Samuel 18:33; 19:2, 4 [b] 1 Kings 1-2 [c] 1 Kings 2:5-9 [d] Acts 13:22

largely found in his repentance. David was a man who, after sinning, would repent to God in earnestness, trusting in God's faithfulness to forgive repentant sinners.

In 2 Samuel 12:13, "David said to Nathan, 'I have sinned against the Lord.'" This repentance is a pattern in David's life. In 2 Samuel 24:10, "David said to the Lord, 'I have sinned greatly in what I have done. But now, O Lord, please take away the iniquity of your servant, for I have done very foolishly.'" In Psalm 51:1–4, David says,

> Have mercy on me, O God, according to your steadfast love; according to your abundant mercy blot out my transgressions. Wash me thoroughly from my iniquity, and cleanse me from my sin! For I know my transgressions, and my sin is ever before me. Against you, you only, have I sinned and done what is evil in your sight, so that you may be justified in your words and blameless in your judgment.

1 Chronicles 21:8 reports, "And David said to God, 'I have sinned greatly in that I have done this thing. But now, please take away the iniquity of your servant, for I have acted very foolishly.'"

David is passionate, and his passion sometimes drives him toward God and other times toward sin. When he sins, he repents from the heart and receives grace from the Lord; however, his sins cause significant pain and peril for both his family and his nation, as the consequences of those sins persist.

Our Faithful God

God was gracious to include David in the lineage of Jesus Christ. Matthew 1 opens, "The book of the genealogy of Jesus Christ, the son of David..." and then closes Jesus' family tree, saying, "So all the generations from Abraham to David were fourteen generations, and from David to the deportation to Babylon fourteen generations, and from the deportation to

Babylon to the Christ fourteen generations."[a] Luke 3 also gives Jesus' genealogy, explaining the family history of Jesus' adoptive father, Joseph, saying, "Jesus, when he began his ministry was about thirty years of age, being the son (as was supposed) of Joseph…" and goes on to say Jesus was "the son of David."[b]

In the Old Testament, God establishes a series of covenants with Noah, Abraham, Moses, and then David. In 2 Samuel 7:8-16, God chooses David to be the next covenant head:

> Thus says the LORD of hosts…I will appoint a place for my people Israel and will plant them, so that they may dwell in their own place and be disturbed no more… Moreover, the LORD declares to you that the LORD will make you a house. When your days are fulfilled and you lie down with your fathers, I will raise up your offspring after you, who shall come from your body, and I will establish his kingdom. He shall build a house for my name, and I will establish the throne of his kingdom forever… And your house and your kingdom shall be made sure forever before me. Your throne shall be established forever.

David was rightly overwhelmed by the gracious covenant promise that not only would a former shepherd boy be a king but also that, from him, would come a King whose Kingdom would endure forever, ruled by none other than the Son of God. David's humble response to God's covenantal grace is reported in 2 Samuel 7:18–19:

> Then King David went in and sat before the LORD and said, "Who am I, O Lord GOD, and what is my house, that you have brought me thus far? And yet this was a small thing in your eyes, O Lord GOD. You have spoken also of your servant's house for a great while to come, and this is instruction for mankind, O Lord GOD!"

God poured a special measure of His grace on Israel

---

[a] Matthew 1:17 [b] Luke 3:23, 31

in the days of David to lift His people to greater heights of dignity. He transformed the nation from a loose confederation of tribes into a strong empire. David, and many of his sons, accomplished much as they ruled over Israel.

Nevertheless, the Old Testament records a sad end for the house of David. The sin of David's sons caused God to remove the throne from Jerusalem. The nation and its king were taken into exile in Babylon. The prophets foretold that a descendant of David would restore the nation.

The New Testament answers these questions by identifying Jesus as the heir of David's throne. Matthew and Luke contain extensive genealogies to demonstrate that Jesus was the promised descendant of David.[a] Jesus was born in Bethlehem, the city of David, as God's providence brought pregnant Mary there to register for a governmental census.[b] As David's final heir, Jesus brings incomparable kingdom blessings to God's covenant people. He fulfills all the hopes of honor associated with the royal line in ways that go exceedingly beyond what David and his other sons accomplished.

The blessings of Christ's Kingdom encompass a vast array of benefits for God's covenant people. To gain a glimpse into what Christ does for us, we will focus on three blessings that came through the line of David during the Old Testament period. Then we will see how Christ brings these gifts to God's people in the New Testament age.

1. David's house was to provide *protection* against evil.
2. The royal line of Judah was to ensure *prosperity* for God's people.
3. David's house was divinely ordained to ensure the special *presence* of God among the people. David spent his life preparing for the temple, a permanent edifice for the presence of God. His son, Solomon, constructed the temple and centered his kingdom on it. The kings of Judah always bore the responsibility of maintaining the proper functioning of the temple. Without the

---

[a] Matthew 1:2-16; Luke 3:23-38 [b] Luke 2:4-6

presence of God, all the efforts of royalty were in vain. There could be no protection or prosperity without the presence of God. The prayers, sacrifices, and songs associated with Israel's temple were the sources out of which all kingdom benefits flowed.

Samuel anointed David as king of Israel[a], but it was many years before he began reigning on the throne.[b] In the meantime, David gathered followers who were loyal to him, influencing life in the kingdom ruled by the evil Saul until the day David began his reign on the throne. In a similar way, after His resurrection and ascension, Jesus rose to the right hand of the Father as anointed King. From that place, He will one day return to earth as reigning king on the historic throne of David. In the meantime, He is gathering faithful followers who will continue the mission to bring people into the glory of the Kingdom. From His exalted position, Jesus bestows Kingdom benefits on the people of God.

Today, we have the firstfruits of the Kingdom, which make us long for the fullness of the Kingdom.[c] While Christ guarantees us spiritual blessings today, His protection, prosperity, and presence will extend even to physical provisions when He returns. Within the new creation, we will be protected against all forms of evil—physical and spiritual.

Thus, Christ inaugurates the fulfillment of all the hopes of the Davidic covenant. He brings the blessings of God's Kingdom to all who serve Him faithfully. David and his sons brought outpourings of tremendous benefits for God's people, but those Old Testament blessings fall short of the dignity for which we were designed and the fullness of God's covenantal grace. Christ alone brings full covenantal Kingdom blessings in His second coming.

Indeed, the Davidic covenant is fulfilled today as the nations come to know Jesus Christ as King of Kings through evangelism and church planting. This explains why the great prayer of Psalm 72 that speaks of Jesus' Kingdom includes this

---

[a] 1 Samuel 16 [b] 2 Samuel 5 [c] Romans 8:23; 1 Cor 15:20-24

echo of the Abrahamic covenant in verse 17: "May his name endure forever, his fame continue as long as the sun! May people be blessed in him, all nations call him blessed!" It is amazing that God's covenant grace is nothing short of a global gift.

Dig Deeper.
1. To learn more about David, read Psalm 51, where David repents of his adultery with Bathsheba and the murder of her husband, Uriah.

Walk it out. Talk it out.
1. What surprises you most about David's faith and failure? Why?
2. What did you learn about the power of repentance by studying the life of David?
3. Who in the story of David's life do you most identify with? (e.g., David, Bathsheba, Uriah, Nathan, Solomon)
4. How can group members be praying for one another this week?

HEBREWS 11

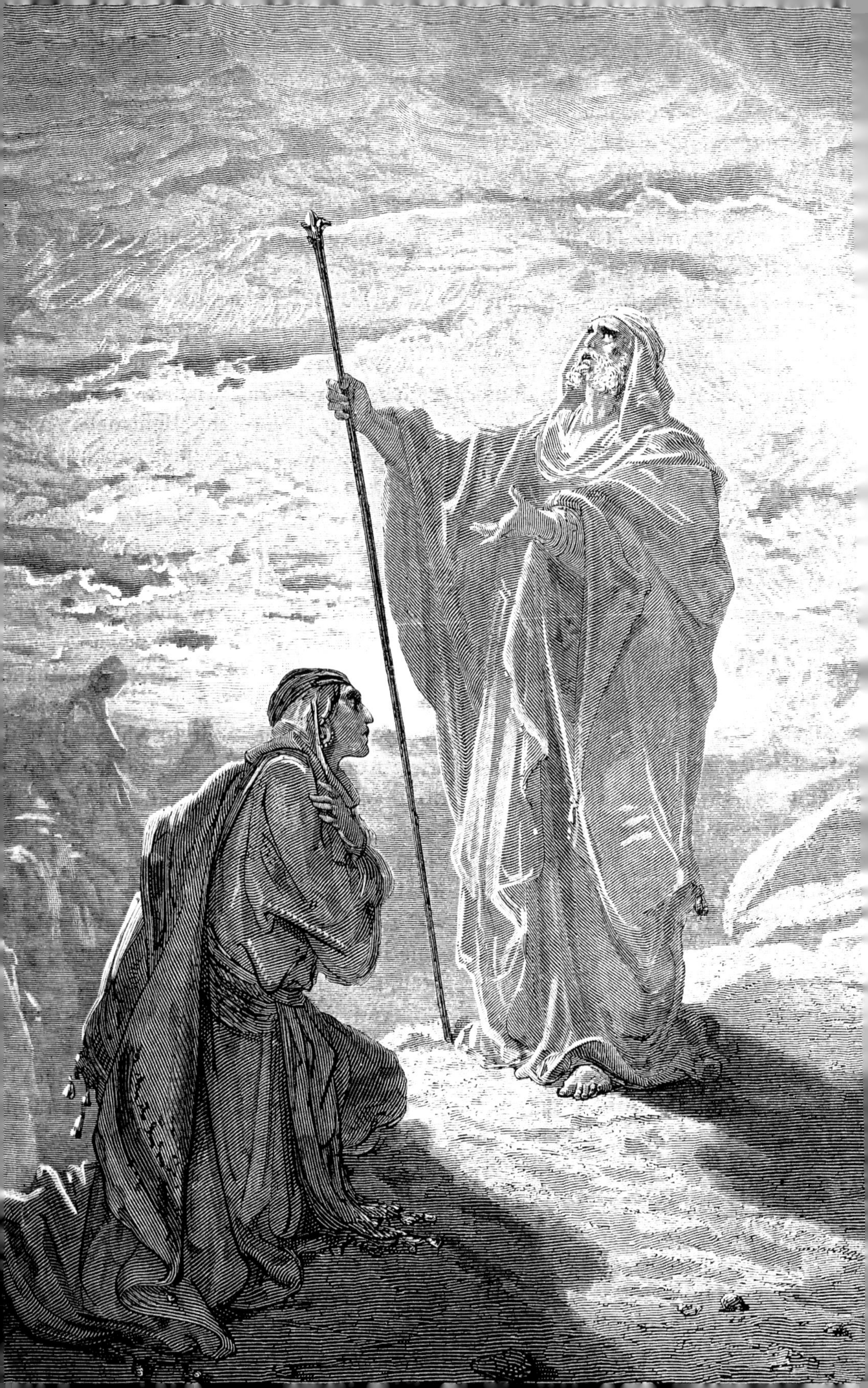

SAMUEL

Chapter 17: Faith for Samuel
Hebrews 11:32

Hebrews 11:32 – And what more shall I say? For time would fail me to tell of…Samuel…

The book of Judges closes with the haunting line, "In those days there was no king in Israel. Everyone did what was right in his own eyes."[a] This vacuum of leadership sets the stage for the birth and leadership of Samuel.

Samuel is a very significant servant of God. A widely respected prophet in Israel, he also served the cause of justice as a judge. He is most famous for helping establish the monarchy in Israel by anointing Saul as its first king and later anointing David as Saul's successor. Throughout his life, Samuel served as a servant of God and leader of the people, continually calling the people to repentance of sin, faith in the Lord, and resistance to Philistine oppression. He serves as a bit of a one-man breach, repeatedly holding back the flood of evil. It is reported that, in response to his preaching and leadership, "the people…put away the Baals and the Ashtaroth, and they served the Lord only."[b]

Samuel's mother, Hannah, was

> Wife of Elkanah from Ephraim's tribe and the mother of the prophet Samuel. The childless Hannah prayed annually at Shiloh for a son, whom she vowed to dedicate to the Lord. The Lord answered her prayer, and she called her son Samuel. When he was weaned (probably about age three), she dedicated him at Shiloh to the service of the Lord in the sanctuary. Henceforth, Samuel lived with Eli the priest and was visited by his parents on their annual pilgrimages. Hannah had three more sons and two daughters (1 Sm 1:1–2:21). Her prophetic psalm (1 Sm 2:1–10) anticipates Mary's song of praise, the "Magnificat" (Lk 1:46–55).[63]

---

[a] Judges 21:25 [b] 1 Samuel 7:4

Samuel's Faith

The summary of Samuel's life is reported in 1 Samuel 1-16. In chapter 1, Samuel is born as an answer to years of prayers from his mother Hannah; he is weaned, and she then hands the boy over to be raised for the Lord's service by Eli, the priest of God. In chapter 2, Hannah sings a prayer in worship to the Lord for her son. In chapters 3-4, Samuel has a vision at the sanctuary and begins his role in the office of prophet. In chapter 4 Eli and his evil sons also die. In chapters 5-7, God's enemies capture the ark and are punished by God, and then the ark is returned to Israel in a battle between the real God and powerful demonic forces. In this season, the people gather under Samuel's leadership, and he is appointed as judge over the entire nation of Israel. In chapter 8, the people are crying out for a king as Samuel's sons are appointed to be spiritual leaders with their father, serving as judges. In chapter 9, King Saul meets with Samuel. In chapter 10, with God's authority, Samuel installs and anoints Saul as the first king in Israel, and Saul receives the Holy Spirit's gift of prophecy. In chapter 11, with God's help, King Saul leads in military victories. In chapter 12, Samuel preaches, telling the people to serve the Lord, and uses his own faithful life as a testimonial example. In chapters 13-14, King Saul sins against God by acting as a priest, which God did not permit, yet he still achieves military victories with the help of his son, Jonathan. In chapter 15, Saul sins against God by failing to exterminate defeated enemies. In chapter 16, Samuel anoints David as the next king, succeeding Saul. From this point onward, the focus largely shifts to King David and Saul's murderous hatred of him, with Samuel fading into the background until his death in 1 Samuel 25.

Samuel's Failure

Samuel was a man of God who served God as a judge in Israel for 28 years, with 18 of those years during the reign of King Saul. He died at the age of 52, and while it is uncertain, he may have written the books of Judges and Ruth. Despite being a man of God, his greatest failure was likely his failure to raise godly sons. 1 Samuel 8:1-5 says,

> When Samuel became old, he made his sons judges over Israel. The name of his firstborn son was Joel, and the name of his second, Abijah; they were judges in Beersheba. Yet his sons did not walk in his ways but turned aside after gain. They took bribes and perverted justice. Then all the elders of Israel gathered together and came to Samuel at Ramah and said to him, "Behold, you are old and your sons do not walk in your ways."

A Bible commentary says,

> It was unusual for a judge to appoint his own sons as judges, for judgeship was not hereditary. In fact, Gideon refused the suggestion that he establish a dynasty; see Judg. 8:22–23.14 Though Eli "judged" (1 Sam. 4:18) Israel for forty years, his sons are never said to have judged. (Their priesthood was of course hereditary.) It may be that the narrator calls the audience's attention to this new development, that is, "a hereditary succession," in the political history of ancient Israel.

It goes on to ponder if Samuel was working on something not decreed by God, namely a "little dynastic experiment." It continues,

> This "experiment" of Samuel's was certainly a breach of the old practice of waiting for the divine appointment of a new judge and was possibly a cause of his family problems. It certainly foreshadows the problems of hereditary kingship in obviating divine choice. It goes on to explain that, the term he appointed…is used again… for "appointing" a king.[64]

It seems possible, if not probable, that Samuel, the great man of God, had a blind spot with his sons. By giving them elevated ministry authority that was not commensurate with their character, he compromised some of his integrity and anointing.

Our Faithful God

Throughout his life, God proves Himself faithful to Samuel. God answers his mother's prayer to have a son and chooses him for ministry from infancy. God appointed Samuel as a prophet during a time when divine revelation was rare in Israel. The Lord began training Samuel through Eli the priest, even beginning to speak to Samuel directly three times as a boy.[a] As Samuel grew, God was with him, ensuring that none of his prophetic words failed to come true. The Lord continued to reveal Himself to Samuel through His word, making him a respected prophet throughout all of Israel as a man who God was with, spoke for, and worked through. Samuel's close relationship with God, nurtured through prayer, allowed him to lead effectively and receive divine guidance in important matters. 1 Samuel 8:6–7 says,

> But the thing displeased Samuel when they said, "Give us a king to judge us." And Samuel prayed to the LORD. And the LORD said to Samuel, "Obey the voice of the people in all that they say to you, for they have not rejected you, but they have rejected me from being king over them."

The people were so certain of the strength of God answering Samuel's prayers that they asked him to inquire of the Lord on their behalf. 1 Samuel 12:19 says, "And all the people said to Samuel, 'Pray for your servants to the Lord your God, that we may not die, for we have added to all our sins this evil, to ask for ourselves a king.'" The man of God responded in 1 Samuel 12:23, saying, "Moreover, as for me, far be it from me that I should sin against the Lord by ceasing to pray for you, and I will instruct you in the good and the right way."

[a] 1 Samuel 2-3

Repeatedly, God heard and answered Samuel's prayers throughout his life. God honored Samuel's faithfulness by establishing him as a powerful spiritual leader, comparable to figures like Moses and Aaron.

Throughout Samuel's life, the secret of his success was that God was with him. 1 Samuel 3:19–21 says,

> And Samuel grew, and the LORD was with him and let none of his words fall to the ground. And all Israel...knew that Samuel was established as a prophet of the LORD. And the LORD appeared again...the LORD revealed himself to Samuel...[and he succeeded] by the word of the LORD.

Samuel is not perfect, but God is present in His life. What is true of Samuel is true of every servant of the Lord—His presence in our life is the only thing that can overcome our imperfections. Samuel was a great man because his great God remained *with* him and *for* him.

Dig Deeper.
1. To learn more about Samuel, read 1 Samuel 1-16.

Walk it out. Talk it out.
1. What surprises you most about the faith and failure of Samuel? Why?
2. What lessons can you learn from the faith of Samuel's parents?
3. Do you know anyone who resembles Samuel a bit—they are used of God to say and do difficult but important things?
4. How can group members be praying for one another this week?

HEBREWS 11

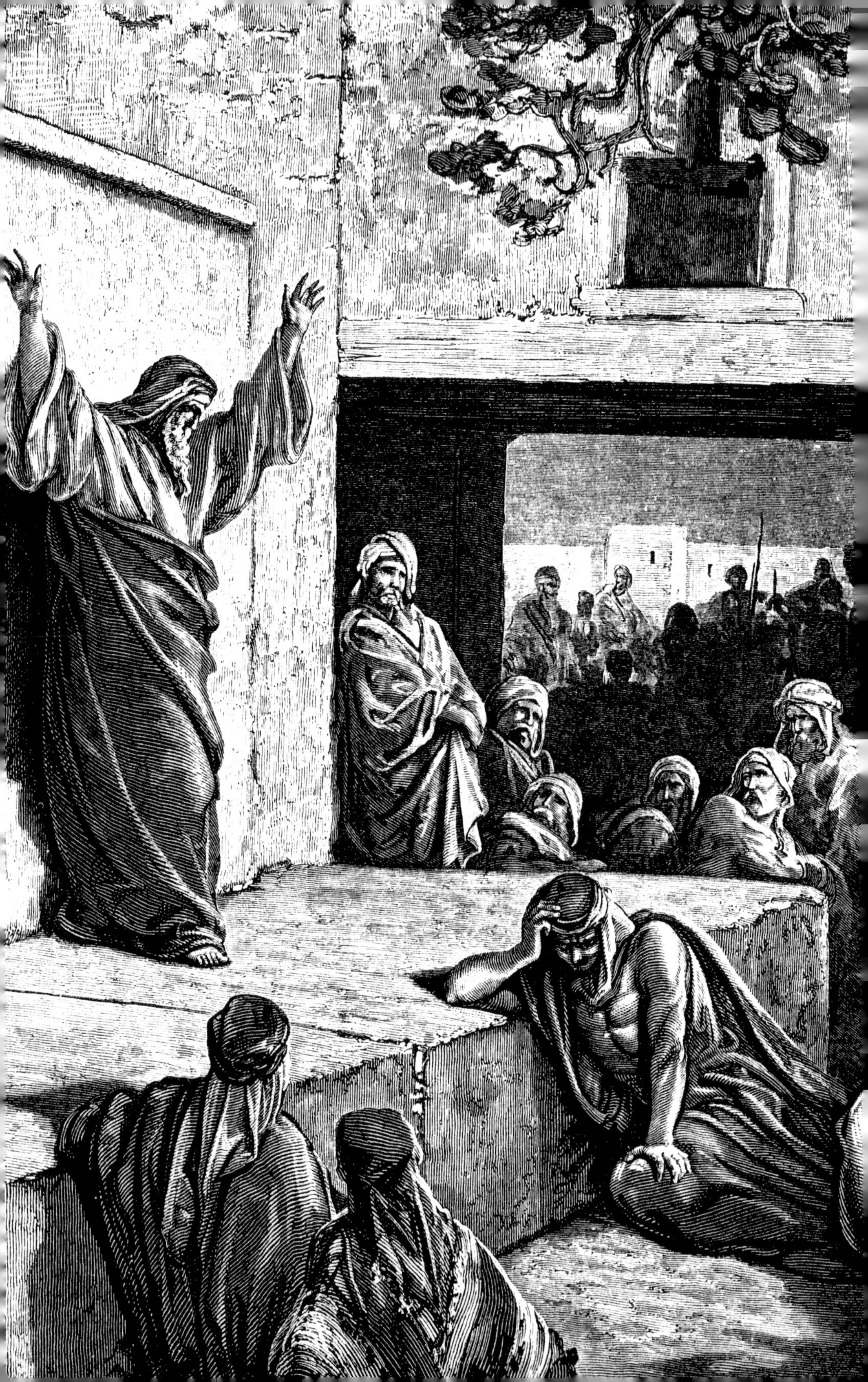

PROPHETS

Chapter 18: Faith for the Prophets
Hebrews 11:32-40

Hebrews 11:32-40 – And what more shall I say? For time would fail me to tell of…the prophets—who through faith conquered kingdoms, enforced justice, obtained promises, stopped the mouths of lions, quenched the power of fire, escaped the edge of the sword, were made strong out of weakness, became mighty in war, put foreign armies to flight. Women received back their dead by resurrection. Some were tortured, refusing to accept release, so that they might rise again to a better life. Others suffered mocking and flogging, and even chains and imprisonment. They were stoned, they were sawn in two, they were killed with the sword. They went about in skins of sheep and goats, destitute, afflicted, mistreated—of whom the world was not worthy—wandering about in deserts and mountains, and in dens and caves of the earth. And all these, though commended through their faith, did not receive what was promised, since God had provided something better for us, that apart from us they should not be made perfect.

As Hebrews 11 nears its close, we read about all the "prophets" of God. A number of terms are used to identify the Old Testament prophets. The title "man of God" refers to the exemplary character and passionate devotion the prophet had for their God.[a] The titles "seer" and "visionary" tend to refer to the prophetic experience of receiving a message from God, either by special insight or visions and dreams.[b] The title "prophet" refers to the office of the person chosen by God to both receive from and communicate for Him.[c] The title "servant of the Lord" indicates the intimate relationship between God and His prophets.[d] The title "messenger of the Lord" refers to the duty of the prophet to speak for God.[e]

In summary, the prophetic calling was the combination of two ministries. First, they received specific revelation directly from God. Second, they spoke the revealed Word to the people

---

[a] Deuteronomy 33:1; 1 Samuel 9:6; 2 Kings 4:9 [b] 1 Samuel 9:9; Amos 7:12; Isaiah 30:10 [c] 1 Samuel 3:20; 1 Kings 18:36; 2 Kings 6:12; Haggai 1:1; Zechariah 1:1 [d] 2 Kings 9:7, 17:13; Jeremiah 7:25; Ezekiel 38:17; Zechariah 1:6 [e] 2 Chronicles 36:15-16; Isaiah 44:26; Haggai 1:13

God had called them to. The prophets were also painfully aware of the weightiness of their call since they consciously knew that they were the very mouth of the Almighty God and spoke for God Himself. For example, this sense of heavy prophetic weight is clearly seen in Moses[a], Isaiah[b], Jeremiah[c], Amos[d], and Zechariah.[e]

The Prophets' Faith

The prophets preached because they were compelled to. Their God instilled His Word so deeply into their hearts and minds that they could do nothing but speak. As Amos said, "The lion has roared; who will not fear? The Lord God has spoken; who can but prophesy?"[f] Perhaps Jeremiah articulated this compulsion best, saying, "But if I say, 'I will not mention him or speak any more in his name,' there is in my heart as it were a burning fire shut up in my bones, and I am weary with holding it in, and I cannot.'"[g]

Indeed, the prophets lived in close intimacy with the Spirit of God. He revealed His Word to them and then empowered them with courage to open their mouths, giving them the words to speak. As a result, one cannot accurately study the prophets without looking around and in them to see the Spirit at work, and one cannot accurately study the prophets without also being filled by the same Spirit that came upon His messengers. According to Old Testament scholar Gerhard von Rad, the phrase "the word of Yahweh" appears 241 times in the Old Testament, including 221 in relation to a prophet.[65] For the prophets, the Word of God was intimate and personal, seizing them and embracing their whole being and not just their intellect.

This is perhaps most graphically displayed in the prophets eating the Word of Yahweh so that it actually became a part of them. To Ezekiel, the Lord said,

---

[a] Exodus 4:16, 7:1-2 [b] Isaiah 1:20 [c] Jeremiah 1:7 [d] Amos 3:8, 7:16 [e] Zechariah 7:12 [f] Amos 3:8 [g] Jeremiah 20:9

"But you, son of man, listen to what I say to you. Do not rebel like that rebellious house; open your mouth and eat what I give you." Then I looked, and I saw a hand stretched out to me, and behold, a scroll of a book was in it. And he spread it before me. And it had writing on the front and on the back, and there were written on it words of lamentation and mourning and woe. And he said to me, "Son of man, eat whatever you find here. Eat this scroll, and go, speak to the house of Israel." So I opened my mouth, and he gave me this scroll to eat. And he said to me, "Son of man, feed your belly with this scroll that I give you and fill your stomach with it." Then I ate it, and it was in my mouth as sweet as honey.[a]

Concerning the Word of God, Jeremiah recorded, "Therefore this is what the Lord God Almighty says: 'Because the people have spoken these words, I will make my words in your mouth a fire and these people the wood it consumes.'"[b] God also said to him, "'Is not my word like fire,' declares the Lord, 'and like a hammer that breaks a rock in pieces?'"[c] God's imagery to Jeremiah is that His Word carries the power of fire on wood and the authority of a hammer on rock. The power of the word of God is perhaps best illustrated by Isaiah: "…my word that goes out from my mouth: It will not return to me empty, but will accomplish what I desire and achieve the purpose for which I sent it."[d]

For the prophets, the Word of God was an extension of God that was so powerful that it could not be overcome by human will. Lastly, the Word of God comes from the objective reference point that God alone occupies and is therefore more certain, true, and real than even our own experiences, perceptions, and speculations.

Unlike priests who were selected by their family origins[e], prophets had only the call of God to legitimize their ministry. Their call was not predicated upon prior ministry testing or

---

[a] Ezekiel 2:8-3:3 [b] Jeremiah 5:14, NIV [c] Jeremiah 23:29, NIV [d] Isaiah 55:11, NIV [e] Exodus 28:1; Leviticus 21-22

ability.[a] The prophetic call seems to include the calling of their name[b], God speaking[c], or the touch of God[d], being seized by God[e], or the Spirit of God coming upon them.[f]

The prophets were largely reformers, demanding immediate repentance and change towards the will and ways of God. When repentance was neglected, they pronounced a death sentence on Israel and led the funeral dirge. However, they knew that God needed to judge, and repentance and mourning had to come and break hardened hearts if a new movement towards salvation was to be birthed. This calling to speak for God against the powers and popularity of the day took incredible faith and came with incredible pain.

The Prophets' Failure

The prophets, too, often struggled with despair, fear, and rejection, just like we do. Moses impulsively struck a rock twice instead of speaking to it as God instructed.[g] Isaiah confessed to having unclean lips.[h] Elijah fled into the wilderness, exhausted and suicidal.[i] Jeremiah was thrown into a cistern and cursed the day of his birth.[j] Jonah ran away from God's calling and was angry with God when grace was poured out on the wicked Ninevites.[k] Balaam took bribes and sought to deceive the nation of Israel.[l] Their categorical inclusion in Hebrews 11 affirms that the faithful are not those without failure but those who continue to act, trust, and suffer in fidelity to God's purposes.

A Bible commentary says, "The final grouping in Hebrews 11:33b–34 references miraculous deliverances: shutting the mouths of lions (likely Daniel), quenching fire (Shadrach, Meshach, and Abednego), and escaping the edge of the sword (e.g., Elijah, Elisha, and David)."[66]

It goes on to say, "But even these acts of faith, filled with power and wonder, are overshadowed by what follows: torture, mocking, flogging, imprisonment, and martyrdom (vv. 35–38). These descriptions evoke the sufferings of…martyrs who refused

[a] Isaiah 6, Hosea 1:2, Jeremiah 1:4-11; Ezekiel 2:1-3:15; Amos 7:14-16 [b] 1 Samuel 3:4) [c] Isaiah 5:9, 22:14; Ezekiel 9:1, 5 [d] 1 Kings 18:46; Ezekiel 8:1 [e] Isaiah 8:11 [f] Numbers 24:2; 2 Kings 3:15 [g] Numbers 20:10-12 [h] Isaiah 6 [i] 1 Kings 19:4 [j] Jeremiah 20:14, 38:6 [k] Jonah 1-4 [l] Numbers 22-24

to renounce the covenant, and of prophets like Isaiah and Zechariah, who were killed for their witness."[67]

Our Faithful God

Roughly 25% of the Bible was prophetic when written, predicting specific details about the future hundreds and thousands of years in advance. No other religion has anything like Bible prophecy, because our Scriptures alone are written by the only God who rules and reveals the future. Repeatedly, God has proven Himself faithful to fulfill the prophecies the Holy Spirit uttered through the prophets. Hundreds of examples could be given, but the following 25 about Jesus Christ from the book *King of Kings* serve to show the faithfulness of God to His Word and that the Bible is all about Jesus!

1. 4000 B.C.: Adam and Eve receive the prophecy that the Messiah (Jesus) would be born of a woman.

Promise: "I will put enmity between you and the woman, and between your offspring and her offspring; he shall bruise your head, and you shall bruise his heel." (Gen. 3:15)

2. 2000 B.C.: Abraham receives the promise that the Messiah (Jesus) would descend from Abraham, through his son Isaac (not Ishmael), Isaac's son Jacob (not Esau), and Jacob's son Judah (not any of the other 11 brothers).

Promise: "...in you [Abraham] all the families of the earth shall be blessed." (Gen. 12:3); "God said... 'Sarah your wife shall bear you a son, and you shall call his name Isaac. I will establish my covenant with him as an everlasting covenant for his offspring after him...'" (Gen. 17:19); "I see him, but not now; I behold him, but not near: a star shall come out of Jacob, and a scepter shall rise out of Israel..." (Num. 24:17); "The scepter shall not depart from Judah, nor the ruler's staff from between his feet, until tribute comes to him; and to him shall be the obedience of the peoples." (Gen. 49:10)

3. 700 B.C.: Isaiah prophesies that Jesus' mother would be a virgin who conceived by a miracle and that Jesus would be God who became a man.

Promise: "Therefore the Lord himself will give you a sign. Behold, the virgin shall conceive and bear a son, and shall call his name Immanuel." (Isa. 7:14)

4. 700 B.C.: Micah prophesies that Jesus would be born in the town of Bethlehem.

Promise: "But you, O Bethlehem Ephrathah, who are too little to be among the clans of Judah, from you shall come forth for me one who is to be ruler in Israel, whose coming forth is from of old, from ancient days [eternity]." (Mic. 5:2)

5. 700 B.C.: Isaiah prophesies that Jesus would live His life without committing any sins.

Promise: "…he had done no violence, and there was no deceit in his mouth." (Isa. 53:9)

6. 700 B.C.: Hosea prophesies that Jesus' family would flee as refugees to Egypt to save His young life.

Promise: "When Israel was a child, I loved him, and out of Egypt I called my son." (Hos. 11:1)

7. 400 B.C.: Malachi prophesies that Jesus would enter the temple. After the temple's destruction in A.D. 70, it no longer existed, making it impossible to fulfill the prophecy any time after that date.

Promise: "Behold, I send my messenger, and he will prepare the way before me. And the Lord whom you seek will suddenly come to his temple; and the messenger of the covenant in whom you delight, behold, he is coming, says the Lord of hosts." (Mal. 3:1)

8. 700 B.C.: Isaiah prophesies that John the Baptizer would prepare the way for Jesus.

Promise: "A voice cries: 'In the wilderness prepare the way of the Lord; make straight in the desert a highway for our God.'" (Isa. 40:3)

9. 700 B.C.: Isaiah prophesies that Jesus would perform many miracles.

Promise: "Then the eyes of the blind shall be opened, and the ears of the deaf unstopped; then shall the lame man leap like a deer, and the tongue of the mute sing for joy." (Isa. 35:5–6)

10. 500 B.C.: Zechariah prophesies that Jesus would ride into Jerusalem on a donkey.

Promise: "Rejoice greatly, O daughter of Zion! Shout aloud, O daughter of Jerusalem! Behold, your king is coming to you; righteous and having salvation is he, humble and mounted on a donkey, on a colt, the foal of a donkey." (Zech. 9:9)

11. 1000 B.C.: David prophesies that Jesus would be betrayed by a friend.

Promise: "Even my close friend in whom I trusted, who ate my bread, has lifted his heel against me." (Ps. 41:9)

12. 500 B.C.: Zechariah prophesies that Jesus' betraying friend would be paid 30 pieces of silver for handing Him over to the authorities and that the payment would be thrown in the temple in disgust (again, the temple was destroyed in A.D. 70, so this prophecy could not have been fulfilled after that time).

Promise: "Then I said to them, 'If it seems good to you, give me my wages; but if not, keep them.' And they weighed out as my wages thirty pieces of silver. Then the Lord said to me, 'Throw it to the potter'—the lordly price at which I was priced by them. So I took the thirty pieces of silver and threw them into the house of the Lord, to the potter." (Zech. 11:12–13)

13. 700 B.C.: Isaiah prophesies that Jesus would be beaten, have His beard plucked out, and be mocked and spit on.

Promise: "I gave my back to those who strike, and my cheeks to those who pull out the beard; I hid not my face from disgrace and spitting." (Isa. 50:6).

14. 1000 B.C.: David prophesies that lots would be cast for Jesus' clothing.

Promise: "…they divide my garments among them, and for my clothing they cast lots." (Ps. 22:18).

15. 700 B.C.: Isaiah prophesies that Jesus would be hated and rejected.

Promise: "He was despised and rejected by men; a man of sorrows, and acquainted with grief; and as one from whom men hide their faces he was despised, and we esteemed him not." (Isa. 53:3)

16. 700 B.C.: Isaiah prophesies that, though hated and rejected, Jesus would not defend Himself.

Promise: "He was oppressed, and he was afflicted, yet he opened not his mouth; like a lamb that is led to the slaughter, and like a sheep that before its shearers is silent, so he opened not his mouth." (Isa. 53:7)

17. 1000 B.C.: David prophesies that Jesus would be crucified (hundreds of years before the invention of crucifixion).

Promise: "For dogs encompass me; a company of evildoers encircles me; they have pierced my hands and feet…" (Ps. 22:16)

18. 700 B.C.: Isaiah prophesies that Jesus would be killed alongside sinners.

Promise: "Therefore I will divide him a portion with the many, and he shall divide the spoil with the strong, because he poured out his soul to death, and was numbered with the transgressors…" (Isa. 53:12)

19. 1400 B.C.: Moses prophesies that none of Jesus' bones would be broken. 1000 B.C.: David prophesies the same.

Promise: "…you shall not break any of [the Passover lamb's] bones." (Ex. 12:46); "He keeps all his bones; not one of them is broken." (Ps. 34:20)

20. 1000 B.C.: David prophesies that Jesus would be forsaken by God.

Promise: "My God, my God, why have you forsaken me? Why are you so far from saving me, from the words of my groaning?" (Ps. 22:1)

21. 700 B.C.: Isaiah prophesies that Jesus would die.

Promise: "…he was cut off out of the land of the living, stricken for the transgression of my people?" (Isa. 53:8b)

22. 700 B.C.: Isaiah prophesies that Jesus would be buried in a tomb given to Him by a rich man.

Promise: "And they made his grave with the wicked and with a rich man in his death, although he had done no violence, and there was no deceit in his mouth." (Isa. 53:9)

23. 1000 B.C.: David prophesies that Jesus would resurrect from death. 700 B.C.: Isaiah prophesies the same.

Promise: "For you will not abandon my soul to Sheol, or let

your holy one see corruption." (Ps. 16:10); "Yet it was the will of the Lord to crush him; he has put him to grief; when his soul makes an offering for guilt, he shall see his offspring; he shall prolong his days; the will of the Lord shall prosper in his hand. Out of the anguish of his soul he shall see and be satisfied; by his knowledge shall the righteous one, my servant, make many to be accounted righteous, and he shall bear their iniquities." (Isa. 53:10–11)

24. *1000 B.C.: David prophesies that Jesus would ascend into Heaven and take the souls of departed Christians with Him.*

Promise: "You ascended on high, leading a host of captives in your train…" (Ps. 68:18)

25. *1000 B.C.: David prophesies that Jesus would sit at the right hand of God.*

Promise: "The Lord says to my Lord: 'Sit at my right hand, until I make your enemies your footstool.'" (Ps. 110:1)

Regarding the prophets and their divine prophecies, a Christian scholar says,

> One of the strongest evidences that the Bible is inspired by God is its predictive prophecy. Unlike any other book, the Bible offers a multitude of specific predictions—some hundreds of years in advance—that have been literally fulfilled or else point to a definite future time when they will come true.

He goes on to quote another scholar, saying he, "lists 1817 predictions in the Bible, 1239 in the Old Testament and 578 in the New."[68]

Over and over, the prophets and their prophecies, along with everyone and everything else in the Bible, keep pointing to Jesus Christ. He alone is the hero of every story in the Bible,

Savior of sinners, Lord over all, center of prophecy and history, and is coming again to rule and reign forever as King of Kings and Lord of Lords!

<u>Keep Looking to Jesus!</u>

In a climactic turn, the author of Hebrews affirms that these heroes were all "commended through their faith," yet "did not receive what was promised…"[a] Their waiting was not in vain, nor were their sufferings without meaning. The closing section of Hebrews 11 looks into the future, far beyond their lifetimes, to the first and second coming of Jesus Christ. Hebrews reminds its readers—and us—that faith is not defined by immediate outcomes but by confidence in God's promises, even when they are deferred. David never saw the everlasting kingdom fully realized in his life; Samuel never witnessed a perfectly obedient king; the prophets died waiting for the new covenant. But all of them bore witness to what was coming. And now, in Christ, their faith, alongside ours, is made perfect.

As we have studied Hebrews 11, I hope you have seen that a faithful servant of God is still flawed. I hope this is an encouragement for you—that God can and does do perfect work through imperfect people and extraordinary things through ordinary people. I am also praying that you will see how their faith did not produce complete results in their life and remember that the same is true for you. It is not until Jesus returns, the dead are raised, the curse is lifted, Heaven and Hell are filled, and Jesus finishes what He started that our faith will become sight.

Until then, we are given very simple instructions to ground our faith in Jesus Christ alone. In the next verses after Hebrews 11, we are directed in 12:2 to keep "looking to Jesus, the founder and perfecter of our faith…" Since we cannot look in two directions at the same time, after being encouraged by the faith of those listed in Hebrews 11, we are exhorted to do as they did—and keep looking to Jesus above and beyond anyone

[a] Heb 11;39

and anything else. They were looking to Jesus, who used their imperfect faith for His perfect plan. We will live by faith, grow in faith, and have our faith eventually become sight if we do the same and keep "looking to Jesus"!

Dig Deeper.

1. To learn more about true versus false prophets, read what Jesus (Matthew 7:15, 24:11, 24), Paul (Acts 20:29-31), and John (1 John 4:1) said. To learn how to discern between true and false prophets, read Deuteronomy 18:14-22 and Jeremiah 23:9-40.

Walk it out. Talk it out.

1. What surprised you most about the faith and failure of the prophets? Why?
2. In this chapter, what big lesson did God give you to apply to your own life?
3. What are the main 1-2 things God taught you in your entire study of Hebrews 11?
4. What is the next step of faith God is asking you to take in your walk with Him?
5. How can group members be praying for each other this week?

ENDNOTES

1. Spurgeon, The Spurgeon Study Bible: Notes (Nashville, TN: Holman Bible Publishers, 2017), 1655.
2. Walter A. Elwell and Philip Wesley Comfort, Tyndale Bible Dictionary, Tyndale Reference Library (Wheaton, IL: Tyndale House Publishers, 2001), 470–471.
3. Paul Ellingworth and Eugene Albert Nida, A Handbook on the Letter to the Hebrews, UBS Handbook Series (New York: United Bible Societies, 1994), 250.
4. C. Spicq, L'Épitre Aux Hébreux (2d ed.; Paris: J. Gabalda, 1952-53), 2. 334.
5. Merland Ray Miller, "What Is the Literary Form of Hebrews 11?," Journal of the Evangelical Theological Society 29, no. 4 (1986): 410.
6. Philip H Hacking, Opening up Hebrews, Opening Up Commentary (Leominster: Day One Publications, 2006), 69.
7. Tom Wright, Hebrews for Everyone (London: Society for Promoting Christian Knowledge, 2004), 127.
8. R. C. H. Lenski, The Interpretation of the Epistle to the Hebrews and of the Epistle of James (Columbus, OH: Lutheran Book Concern, 1938), 372.
9. Erik M. Heen and Philip D. W. Krey, eds., Hebrews, Ancient Christian Commentary on Scripture (Downers Grove, IL: InterVarsity Press, 2005), 172.
10. George Guthrie, Hebrews, The NIV Application Commentary (Grand Rapids, MI: Zondervan Publishing House, 1998), 373.
11. NIV Bible Speaks Today: Notes (London: IVP, 2020), 1684
12. Luke Timothy Johnson, Hebrews: A Commentary, ed. C. Clifton Black, M. Eugene Boring, and John T. Carroll, 1st ed., The New Testament Library (Louisville, KY: Westminster John Knox Press, 2012), 274.
13. Joseph S. Exell, The Biblical Illustrator: Hebrews, vol. 2 (London: James Nisbet & Co., n.d.), 184–185.
14. Donald K. McKim, The Westminster Dictionary of Theological Terms, Second Edition, Revised and Expanded

15. (Louisville, KY: Westminster John Knox Press, 2014), 274.
15. Henry Hampton Halley, Halley's Bible Handbook with the New International Version., Completely rev. and expanded. (Grand Rapids, MI: Zondervan Publishing House, 2000), 863–864.
16. Douglas Mangum, The Lexham Glossary of Theology (Bellingham, WA: Lexham Press, 2014).
17. L., "Presuppositionalism," in Dictionary of Christianity in America (Downers Grove, IL: InterVarsity Press, 1990).
18. Tom Wright, Hebrews for Everyone (London: SPCK, 2004), 128.
19. Thomas D. Lea, Hebrews, James, vol. 10, Holman New Testament Commentary (Nashville, TN: Broadman & Holman Publishers, 1999), 200.
20. Erik M. Heen and Philip D. W. Krey, eds., Hebrews, Ancient Christian Commentary on Scripture (Downers Grove, IL: InterVarsity Press, 2005), 175–176.
21. Lesley Difranco, "Sacrifice," in Lexham Theological Wordbook.
22. David Atkinson, The Message of Genesis 1–11: The Dawn of Creation, ed. J. A. Motyer and Derek Tidball, The Bible Speaks Today (England: Inter-Varsity Press, 1990), 127–128.
23. James Montgomery Boice, Genesis: An Expositional Commentary (Grand Rapids, MI: Baker Books, 1998), 287.
24. Leland Ryken et al., Dictionary of Biblical Imagery (Downers Grove, IL: InterVarsity Press, 2000), 922–923.
25. D. A. Neal, "Enoch," in The Lexham Bible Dictionary, ed. John D. Barry et al. (Bellingham, WA: Lexham Press, 2016).
26. https://www.collinsdictionary.com/us/dictionary/english/pseudepigrapha
27. D. A. Neal, "Enoch," in The Lexham Bible Dictionary, ed. John D. Barry et al. (Bellingham, WA: Lexham Press, 2016).
28. Richard R. Losch, All the People in the Bible: An A–Z Guide to the Saints, Scoundrels, and Other Characters in Scripture (Grand Rapids, MI; Cambridge, U.K.: William B. Eerdmans Publishing Company, 2008), 107.
29. Robert Masson Boyd, "ENOCH," in A Dictionary of the Bible: Dealing with Its Language, Literature, and Contents

Including the Biblical Theology, ed. James Hastings et al. (New York; Edinburgh: Charles Scribner's Sons; T. & T. Clark, 1911–1912), 705.
30. Leland Ryken et al., Dictionary of Biblical Imagery (Downers Grove, IL: InterVarsity Press, 2000), 922–923.
31. P. E. Enns, "Grumbling," in New Dictionary of Biblical Theology, ed. T. Desmond Alexander and Brian S. Rosner, electronic ed. (Downers Grove, IL: InterVarsity Press, 2000), 527.
32. https://www.ifcj.org/news/stand-for-israel-blog/discovering-joshuas-tomb
33. https://biblearchaeologyreport.com/2019/05/25/biblical-sites-three-discoveries-at-jericho/
34. Bible Review (Biblical Archaeology Society, 2004).
35. Ibid.
36. H. L. Willmington, Willmington's Bible Handbook (Wheaton, IL: Tyndale House Publishers, 1997), 862.
37. Robert G. Bratcher and Howard A. Hatton, A Handbook on Deuteronomy, UBS Handbook Series (New York: United Bible Societies, 2000), 388.
38. Robert G. Bratcher and Howard A. Hatton, A Handbook on Deuteronomy, UBS Handbook Series (New York: United Bible Societies, 2000), 388.
39. Douglas K. Stuart, Exodus, vol. 2 of The New American Commentary (Nashville: Broadman & Holman Publishers, 2006), 725.
40. Both Jewish and Christian interpreters have famously attempted to sanitize this story by seeing Rahab's establishment as an inn and Rahab as the innkeeper. See, for example, Josephus, Jewish Antiquities 5.1.2.
41. Bible Review (Biblical Archaeology Society, 2004).
42. Michael Green, The Message of Matthew: The Kingdom of Heaven, The Bible Speaks Today (Leicester, England; Downers Grove, IL: InterVarsity Press, 2001), 58.
43. Brown, Raymond. The Message of Hebrews: Christ Above All. The Bible Speaks Today. Downers Grove, IL: InterVarsity Press, 1988, pg. 212.
44. Leon Morris, The Gospel according to Matthew, The Pillar

New Testament Commentary (Grand Rapids, MI; Leicester, England: W.B. Eerdmans; Inter-Varsity Press, 1992), 23.
45. Tikva S. Frymer-Kensky, "Rahab," in The HarperCollins Bible Dictionary (Revised and Updated), ed. Mark Allan Powell (New York: HarperCollins, 2011), 864.
46. Leland Ryken et al., Dictionary of Biblical Imagery (Downers Grove, IL: InterVarsity Press, 2000), 112.
47. Robert B. Hughes and J. Carl Laney, Tyndale Concise Bible Commentary, The Tyndale Reference Library (Wheaton, IL: Tyndale House Publishers, 2001), 96.
48. Brandon Grafius, "Deborah the Judge," ed. John D. Barry et al., The Lexham Bible Dictionary (Bellingham, WA: Lexham Press, 2016).
49. David Noel Freedman, Allen C. Myers, and Astrid B. Beck, "Crescents," ed. David Noel Freedman, Allen C. Eerdmans Dictionary of the Bible (Grand Rapids, MI: W.B. Eerdmans, 2000), 295.
50. Terry L. Brensinger, Judges, Believers Church Bible Commentary (Scottdale, PA: Herald Press, 1999), 101.
51. Arthur S. Peake, "CHEMOSH," in A Dictionary of the Bible: Dealing with Its Language, Literature, and Contents Including the Biblical Theology, ed. James Hastings et al. (New York; Edinburgh: Charles Scribner's Sons; T. & T. Clark, 1911–1912), 376.
52. Lesley DiFransico, "Women in the Bible, Mistreatment of," in The Lexham Bible Dictionary, ed. John D. Barry et al. (Bellingham, WA: Lexham Press, 2016).
53. Michael Wilcock, The Message of Judges: Grace Abounding, ed. J. A. Motyer and Derek Tidball, The Bible Speaks Today (England: Inter-Varsity Press, 1992), 16.
54. Adam L. Myers, "Philistines," ed. John D. Barry et al., The Lexham Bible Dictionary (Bellingham, WA: Lexham Press, 2016).
55. Jay Todd, "Samson the Judge," ed. John D. Barry et al., The Lexham Bible Dictionary (Bellingham, WA: Lexham Press, 2016).
56. Adam L. Myers, "Philistines," ed. John D. Barry et al., The Lexham Bible Dictionary (Bellingham, WA: Lexham Press,

2016).
57. Leland Ryken et al., Dictionary of Biblical Imagery (Downers Grove, IL: InterVarsity Press, 2000), 755.
58. Terry Hall, The Old Testament Express (Wheaton, IL: Victor Books: A Division of SP Publications, Inc., 1985), 114.
59. Rolf A. Jacobson, Karl N. Jacobson, and Hans H. Wiersma, eds., "David," in Crazy Book: A Not-So-Stuffy Dictionary of Biblical Terms (Minneapolis, MN: Fortress Press, 2019), 61.
60. David M. Howard Jr., "David (Person)," in The Anchor Yale Bible Dictionary, ed. David Noel Freedman (New York: Doubleday, 1992), 41.
61. Rolf A. Jacobson, Karl N. Jacobson, and Hans H. Wiersma, eds., "David," in Crazy Book: A Not-So-Stuffy Dictionary of Biblical Terms (Minneapolis, MN: Fortress Press, 2019), 61.
62. David M. Howard Jr., "David (Person)," in The Anchor Yale Bible Dictionary, ed. David Noel Freedman (New York: Doubleday, 1992), 41.
63. Walter A. Elwell and Philip Wesley Comfort, Tyndale Bible Dictionary, Tyndale Reference Library (Wheaton, IL: Tyndale House Publishers, 2001), 571.
64. David Tsumura, The First Book of Samuel, The New International Commentary on the Old Testament (Grand Rapids, MI: Wm. B. Eerdmans Publishing Co., 2007), 245.
65. Carl F. H. Henry, God, Revelation, and Authority (Wheaton, IL: Crossway Books, 1999), 423.
66. Attridge, Harold W., and Helmut Koester. The Epistle to the Hebrews: A Commentary on the Epistle to the Hebrews. Hermeneia—a Critical and Historical Commentary on the Bible. Philadelphia: Fortress Press, 1989. Pg. 349
67. Attridge, Harold W., and Helmut Koester. The Epistle to the Hebrews: A Commentary on the Epistle to the Hebrews. Hermeneia—a Critical and Historical Commentary on the Bible. Philadelphia: Fortress Press, 1989. Pg. 350
68. Norman L. Geisler, "Prophecy, as Proof of the Bible," in Baker Encyclopedia of Christian Apologetics, Baker Reference Library (Grand Rapids, MI: Baker Books, 1999), 609.